The Saturday Book

Thirty-first Year

The Saturday Book

EDITED BY JOHN HADFIELD

31

Clarkson N. Potter, Inc./Publisher   NEW YORK

DISTRIBUTED BY CROWN PUBLISHERS, INC.

THE SATURDAY BOOK was founded in 1941 by Leonard Russell and has been edited since 1952 by John Hadfield. This thirty-first annual issue has been made and printed in Great Britain by The Anchor Press Ltd, Tiptree, Essex.

Library of Congress Catalog Card Number: 42-51009

Inquiries should be addressed to Clarkson N. Potter, Inc., 419 Park Avenue South, New York 10016.

First American edition published 1971 by Clarkson N. Potter, Inc., New York.

The frontispiece reproduces a detail from 'Punch or May Day' by Benjamin Robert Haydon, 1829 (Tate Gallery, London). The engravings reproduced on the half-title page and pages 168, 171, 182 and 200 are from *The Fly*, 1839.

Introduction

GLANCING THROUGH an antiquarian bookseller's cata-
logue the other day we observed that a complete run of
the thirty issues of THE SATURDAY BOOK was being
offered for £75·00 or $180·00 (and a good bargain it was, judging by
the prices usually asked nowadays for individual volumes). It
occurred to us then that an interesting and appropriate subject
for one of those remembrances-of-things-past which fill so many
of our pages would be the early history of THE SATURDAY BOOK
itself.

How many of today's readers have ever seen a copy of that first
(unnumbered) issue which was devised by Leonard Russell thirty
years ago as solace for a war-weary world? It was a beautifully
designed book, with some distinguished contributors, but quite
different in character and appearance from the book which you
are now reading. It had a certain air of *belles lettres* that is now
suggestive of the 'thirties—even the 'twenties. The element of
social commentary, and the 'scrap-book' type of presentation,
did not emerge until the third issue, published in 1943, which was
half as thick as the first issue, and was printed on that kind of
buff wrapping paper that war-time economy required. Scruffy as
that book appears to the modern eye it nevertheless opened with
a very lively series of photographs illustrating social changes of
the past hundred years. The SATURDAY BOOK formula was
germinating.

The fourth number saw an extraordinary change. The pictorial
section expanded to 128 pages, of which fourteen were printed in
colour. This was probably THE SATURDAY BOOK's 'finest hour',
a resplendent gesture of lavish extravagance in a year dominated
by scarcity, drabness and austerity. No wonder the sales rocketed.

There is no room to continue the Saturdiurnal Saga here—
though we shall do so one day. But it is interesting to observe
certain similarities between those early volumes and that which
you now hold in your hand. In the very first volume the illustrations were almost all wood-engravings made specially for the
book by Agnes Miller Parker. This is a tradition that has been
maintained. In mid-career we presented some lovely examples

of the work of the late Robert Gibbings. In our last two issues we printed engravings by that modern master, George Mackley. In this issue we introduce a distinguished but less well-known engraver, Monica Poole.

A feature of that notable fourth number was a series of photographs by a then unknown photographer, Edwin Smith. His work —with essays by his wife, Olive Cook—has been represented in every issue since then.

Obviously a lot of the character of the early SATURDAY BOOKS derived from the fact that their editor, Leonard Russell, had stumbled upon and acquired a large collection of curious Victorian photographs. Many of these have now become familiar through reproduction in other books. Industrious picture researchers have, during the past thirty years, explored almost every library, archive and junk shop where Victorian photographs can be found. Yet we are still able to discover such visual treasure trove as Mr Philip Kaplan's wonderful collection of nineteenth-century cabinet photos, of which some choice examples are reproduced in this number.

Though we doubt if any of those early issues offered anything as dazzlingly 'new' as Andrew Grima's jewelled watches, the mixture is still very largely 'as before'. We fondly hope that in a world of ever-shifting values, at the mercy of instant fashions and ephemeral fads, you can continue to *rely* upon THE SATURDAY BOOK—for the usual assortment of the unusual.

J.H.

For permission to quote the passages from Kilvert's *Diary* on pages 172 and 178 acknowledgement is made to the Estate of Mrs G. J. K. Fletcher, Mr William Plomer, Messrs. Jonathan Cape, and the Macmillan Company, New York.

Contents

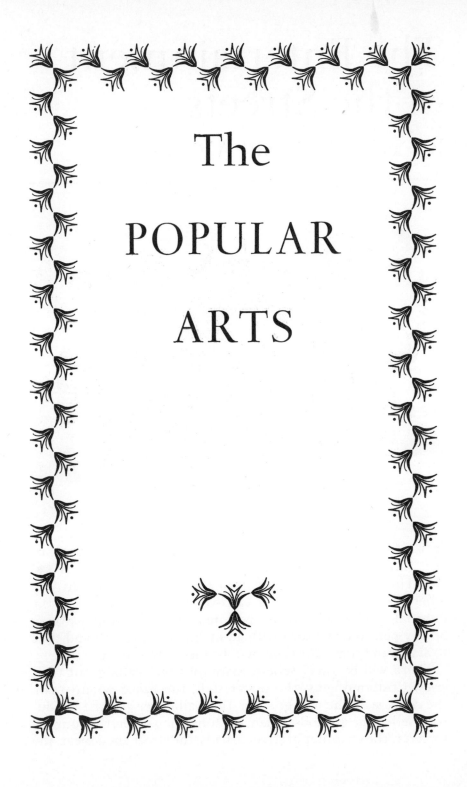

The

POPULAR

ARTS

The Entertainment of the Streets

BY GEORGE SPEAIGHT

LET US STEP into the street. The city may be London or
Paris or Rome or Munich or Vienna or Boston or New York.
The year may be 1900 or 1800 or 1700 or even 1600. Any city
where civilised urban life is carried on. Any year before the
internal-combustion engine polluted the land. And we may
be any person or persons with an inclination to stroll and time
to stand and stare. For there will be plenty to stare at.

There will be street sellers, many of them calling out their
cries. Costermongers, the oyster stall, the baked-potato man,
the coffee stall, the orange seller, the wallflower girl, the Hindu-
tract seller, the groundsel man, the long-song seller, the running
patterer, the chaunter of street ballads, the street auctioneer, the

corn curer, the street herbalist, the grease remover, the lucifer-match girl, the Tyrolean broom girl, the sweep, the old-clothes man, the plaster-image boy ...

There will be beggars. Distressed operatives, frozen-out gardeners, starved-out workmen in aprons and paper caps; disaster beggars, shipwrecked mariners, blown-up miners, burnt-out tradesmen; turnpike sailors and wounded soldiers; destitute Poles, Negroes and Indians ...

Whether we buy or not, whether we bestow a coin here or there, these street sellers and beggars are, at least, providing value for any money we spend. Every seller does his best to gather a crowd and extol the virtues of his wares in terms of hyperbole; every beggar—genuine or bogus—puts on a show to wring our hearts. The streets, indeed, provide one vast entertainment for those with time to enjoy it. And then there are the street entertainers themselves ...

Here is a group of men with blackened faces and horse-hair wigs, dressed in 'plantation costumes', twanging banjos, banging tambourines and knocking the bones. They are the 'Nigger Minstrels', already beginning to think it more euphonious to call themselves the Ethiopian Serenaders. The germ of this idea was conceived by an American actor called T. D. Rice, who swept two countries with a song called 'Jim Crow' in which he reproduced upon the stage the antics of a Negro street performer he had seen in Cincinatti. Rice's example led to a host of imitators—white artists dressed up as Negroes and singing supposedly Negro songs. There were the Virginia Minstrels, who launched this kind of entertainment in New York in 1843; the Ethiopian Serenaders, headed by the banjoist Pell, who arrived in England in 1846; the Christy Minstrels in 1857; and many others. And modest itinerant troupes were performing on the streets almost as soon as the vogue arrived.

They may be singing 'Buffalo Gals', 'Lucy Neale' or 'O Susannah'. There is a song called 'Going ober de Mountain' with a 'symphony' on the bones between every line; these bones were rib-of-beef bones (artificial ebony bones were very grand but sounded even better), and required hard practice to play well; they could bring the skin off the performer's fingers. In between the songs there will be a dialogue between the leader of the troupe and his men:

'Mister Tambo, can you tell me how to spell blind pig in two letters?'

'Why no, I can't tell dat.'

'Why it's simple, Mister Tambo. P, g, 'cos if you leave the i out it must be a blind pig! Ha ha ha! And now we go on wid de consort.'

And the troupe launches into a rendering of 'Mary Blane'.

Here is a team of stilt walkers—a mother and two little girls, under eight years of age. The mother is a skilled artiste; she unstraps one stilt, shoulders it like a gun, and goes through the actions of handling it in exercise, all the time standing upon one stilt. She can walk on stilts as high as the first floor of a house and look in at the windows—a very effective way of coaxing a coin from the surprised people inside. Her daughters dance waltzes and polkas. They have been trained to walk on stilts from the age of two and a half and were performing in public a year later. Their father, if we ask him how they were taught, will tell us: 'My little things took to it almost naturally. It was bred and born in them. . . . They would put them on for play.' But he hints darkly that not all children have been trained so humanely. 'Some people, when they teach their children for any entertainment, torture the little things most dreadful. There is a great deal of barbarity practised in teaching children for the various lines. It's very silly, because it only frightens the little things and some children often will do much more by kindness than ill-usage.'

This enlightened and happy family is only performing in the streets as a stop-gap between profitable engagements at circuses or fairs. But let us pass on, for here is another performer making his pitch.

He is a conjurer who has set up a portable table covered with a fringed cloth of black velvet. He is dressed in ballet shirt and braces with spangled tights and fleshlings. He is doing card tricks, identifying any card selected by a spectator. Then he throws a pack in the air and catches the selected card on the point of a sword.

If we can take the conjurer aside after the collection and can persuade him to reveal how it is all done he will tell us that tricks like 'sautez-le-coup', which he has just performed, are

Street conjurer: engraving from Mayhew's *London Labour and the London Poor*, 1851

'feats of great dexterity and quickness of hand'. He skins his finger at the end to make it highly sensitive, and pricks the selected card in the corner with a concealed pin. He can tell, by touch, a pricked card in a moment. The greatest art, he will tell us, is 'forcing, that is, making a party take the card you wish him to; and let him try ever so well, he will have it, though he's not conscious of it'.

Another effective trick, if he sees a gentleman in the crowd, is to borrow a sovereign, wrap it in a handkerchief, and give it to its owner to hold. 'Now, my Lord, are you sure you hold it?' he asks. 'Yes, old fellow.' 'Now, my Lord, if I was to take the sovereign away from you without you knowing it, wouldn't you say I was perfectly welcome to it?' 'Yes, old fellow, go on.' When the handkerchief is opened there is only a farthing in it!

Magical effects were preceded by the mystic incantation: 'Albri kira mumma tousha cocus co shiver de freek from the margin under the crippling hook.' (A philologist could write a book about the origins and transformations of these words.)

Some conjurers—though surely not the obliging old performer who has revealed his secrets to us—practised thimble-rigging. This is a version of the famous sleight-of-hand trick called the 'cup and balls'. Three thimbles are placed on the table and a pea is moved from under one to the other in a series of rapid passes. Someone in the audience is invited to say under which thimble it is and to back his choice with a bet. He is nearly always wrong. Before we get too disheartened the conjurer's attention is distracted, causing him to turn his back on the table; a joker in the crowd seizes the opportunity to lift a thimble to show the pea under it. On the conjurer then inviting bets, someone in the crowd is sure to stake all he has on the thimble under which he has seen the pea. The conjurer accepts his money, but when the punter lifts the designated thimble there is nothing there!

The trick is, of course, done with the aid of confederates in the crowd, one of whom makes the diversion and the other lifts the thimble, secreting the pea, however, as he replaces it. A second pea has usually already been placed under one of the other thimbles, to be revealed in due course.

But let us return to the honest entertainments of the streets, of which there is no lack. Here is a 'school' of five acrobats. They have quite a range of postures to strike: 'the pyramid' is three men high; 'the Arabs hang down' consists of a man standing on the base or 'strong man's' shoulder, while a third hangs face down from his neck; 'the spread' consists of a man on the strong man's shoulders, with a third and fourth hanging from each hand; for 'the Hercules' the strong man kneels on hands and knees, two men stand on his back, and the fourth balances on their shoulders. The 'perche' is a long fir pole held in a socket in the strong man's waistband, while a light and agile member, called 'the sprite', runs up the pole and strikes attitudes at the top with other fancy names, like 'the bottle', 'the horizontal' and 'the hanging down by one toe'. He, too, has the advantage of being able to look into first-floor windows.

But what sound is this? The beating of a drum, the high flute-like call of the pandean pipes, and a shrill unintelligible squeaking sets all the loungers and a host of children hastening towards the narrow booth from which these cries emanate. It is a Punch and Judy show. Punch, grotesquely hook-nosed and hunch-backed, throws his Baby out of the window; and then meets Judy's tirades with enough blows of his stick to knock her lifeless; he similarly dispatches the Beadle, the Black Man and the Doctor; he counts and miscounts the corpses with the aid, and hindrance, of Joey the Clown; he is scared by the Ghost of Judy and by the Crocodile; he is taken to be hanged by the Hangman, but tricks him into putting his head into his own noose; and finally he defeats the Devil himself in an exchange of slapsticks.

This enchanting puppet show originated in Italy, with Pulcinella a black-masked, white-smocked character from the Commedia dell' Arte. The Pulcinella show may still be seen in Italy with a drama similar to, but not at all identical with, that of Punch. As it travelled across Europe it acquired distinct national characteristics wherever it took root. Punch arrived in England in 1662 (an inscription under the portico of St Paul's Church, Covent Garden, records the date and the place), but it was not till towards the end of the eighteenth century that the now familiar glove puppet show, performed by one man

with a puppet on each hand, became established as a street entertainment in London.

No one knows quite how this traditional drama came to be formed. Some of the elements are clearly medieval survivals; some are of Italian origin; but most of the characters have an English background, and the play must have just shaped itself

Punch and Judy: drawing by Gustave Doré, 1872

on the fingers of hungry showmen from the laughter of street urchins. Punch at one time, in the seventeenth and eighteenth centuries, appeared as a ubiquitous clown in any number of different plays, as do his foreign counterparts, Guignol and Kasperl, to this day; but once the Punch and Judy show was established in the streets it hardly varied in its plot. It is, indeed, admirably adapted for the purpose of open-air performance.

Pulcinella show: Italian nineteenth-century lithograph

Peepshow. 'The Show': mezzotint by J. Young
after a painting by John Hoppner, R.A. (1758–1810)

Pulcinella show: engraving by Pinelli, 1815

Another kind of show that will solicit our custom is the peep-show. This consists, basically, of a box with a number of eye-pieces in which lenses are fitted. Inside the box hang painted scenes which may be brought into view by pulling or releasing cords on the outside. A lamp may illuminate the interior or the lid be raised to admit the daylight. The scenes displayed within usually depict battles, sensational murders or scenes from popular plays. The battle of Waterloo and the death of Nelson are great favourites. The whole thing is small enough to be carried on a man's back and set up on trestles.

And now another note strikes our ears—the wail of the bagpipes. The player stands at a street corner, while on the ground beside him a pair of little puppets dance and jig in time to the music. Careful examination reveals a string passing from the musicians' knee, or foot, to a short vertical post set at the end of a horizontal plank on which the puppets are dancing. This string passes through the puppets' bodies at chest height. As the musician slackens or tightens the string, the puppets respond by jerking their limbs and bodies in some semblance of a jig.

Indeed, the accidental jerks of these *marionnettes à la planchette* possess a charm that the most elaborately articulated marionettes often lose. These jigging puppets were carried all over Europe, and have been recorded by dozens of delightful *genre* prints and sketches; often, instead of the bagpipe player, an almond-eyed Savoyard boy plays on a pipe or turns the handle of a hurdy-gurdy as the puppets advance towards each other to the culmination of a final collision-embrace.

An altogether more imposing kind of puppet show is presented by the Fantoccini in an ornate booth whose architect seems to have been a disciple of Mr Pugin. Like Punch and Judy, this is accompanied upon the drum and panpipes by a gentleman called 'the bottler' who also takes up the collection. But this show is performed by marionettes worked by strings from above, who really show to greater advantage on a larger stage.

Jigging puppets: detail from 'Southwark Fair', after Hogarth, 1733

Fantoccini show: engraving after George
Cruikshank from Hone's *Every-Day Book*, 1825

However, even in these cramped conditions some remarkable
tricks are performed: a Nondescript takes his head off and
juggles with it; a skeleton's limbs separate from its trunk and
dance independently in the four corners of the stage before
reuniting; a Grand Turk waddles on, his arms and legs drop off
to be transformed into children and the body turns upside down
to become their mother who leads them in crocodile off the
stage; or another variant of the same effect shows an old lady's
limbs dropping off to become little people, her body turns into
a balloon, the people jump into the basket and they sail away.

Mechanical figures. 'The Showman': early nineteenth-century engraving

And here are the Mechanical Figures. These move not by any direct control from the showman but by mechanism activated as he turns a handle. They may represent people at work on various trades, or dancers or musicians; or they may show little scenes from history or the Bible. An Italian showman described his display as follows: 'I have three leetle figuers to this box: one is Judith cutting the head of the infidel chief—what you call him?—Holofernes. She lift her arm with the sword, and she roll her eyes, and the other hand is on his head, which it lifts. . . . There is another figuer of the soldat which mounts the guard; the soldat goes to sleep, and his head falls on his bosom; then he wake again and lift his lance and roll his eyes; then he goes to sleep again. . . . The other figuer is of the lady with the plate in the hand, and she make salutation to the company for to ask some money, and she continue to do this so long as anybody giver her money.'

And all the time as the handle turns the music plays. There have been many forms of mechanical music in the streets. The hurdy-gurdy, a term often inaccurately applied to all mechanical

Old Sarah, a hurdy-gurdy player well-known in mid-nineteenth-century London: an engraving from a daguerrotype, reproduced by Mayhew

street instruments, is a musical instrument with a very respectable history going back to the twelfth century. Indeed, it cannot correctly be described as mechanical music at all, though it was popular with the humblest street musicians up to the middle of the nineteenth century. It is a six- or seven-stringed instrument fitted with a wheel in contact with the strings that is turned by a handle outside the case; four of the strings are so arranged that so long as the wheel turns they are sounded continuously on an unvarying note, producing a drone effect similar to bagpipes. The remaining two or three strings are also sounded continuously by the turning wheel, but their notes can be varied by finger-operated keys to produce a melody.

The barrel organ, properly so described, is—as its name implies—a wind-operated instrument. Turning the handle works a pair of bellows which force air through the pipes and also turns a pinned cylinder or barrel which opens or closes apertures into the selected pipes, thus producing the desired tune. One barrel might play eight different tunes by a slight lateral shift between each tune, bringing a fresh set of pins into contact with the mechanism that opens the apertures of the pipes. The case is slung by a leather strap over the 'grinder's' shoulder. This

Barrel pianos. 'The Rival Operas': mid-nineteenth-century engraving

is the instrument being played to accompany the stilt walkers in the print reproduced on page 13.

The barrel organ was generally replaced in the second half of the nineteenth century by the portable barrel piano, which, however, took over the old name in common parlance. This basically consists of a piano-type harp, mounted vertically, of some twenty-two strings struck by hammers activated from pins set in a barrel that is turned by a handle outside the case. There may be some ten different tunes on one barrel, which can be changed as required for a new set of tunes. This instrument is also usually carried by a leather strap over the grinder's shoulder, and is supported when in use by a vertical pole. Sometimes automaton figures are fitted on the case and the showmen often train a monkey, dressed perhaps as a soldier, to do tricks on the top.

The barrel piano had been replaced by the street piano by the end of the nineteenth century. This instrument, still sometimes to be heard in London streets, is of orthodox upright pianoforte construction and may have from forty to fifty-five notes and play ten tunes on each barrel. Its increased size makes it necessary to fit it with wheels. Until quite recently a number of Italian firms in Clerkenwell used to hire these instruments out by the day, and until his death in 1959 the late Canon Wintle, an admirable clergyman in Suffolk, restored a great many street pianos for the use of charitable organisations.

Some worthy British citizens were driven almost mad by all this street music. The New Police Act of 1839 tried to regulate it (but the Punch men were defended in the House of Lords from its harsh imposition upon their performances); the Metropolitan Police Act of 1864 (still in force) tried to suppress it. Notices in London squares may still be seen proclaiming: 'No Street Noises, Hawkers' Cries or Organs—By Order.' A New York City Ordinance forbad the use of street pianos as recently as 1934. But street music and street entertainment would have survived all this if they had not been driven off the streets by a monster who drowned their tunes and cries in the nerve-shattering roar in which our lives are submerged today.

Here and there a pavement artist will still chalk his salmon sunsets, or a Punch and Judy will still play on the edge of a common, or an escapologist will still call for ten more sportsmen to throw down their silver coins before he releases himself from his strait-jacket. The tradition of street entertainment is not quite dead, though sadly diminished. But, at least, we can

Street piano with mechanical figures. 'The Monster Organ': engraving from *The Illustrated London News*, 1846

still step into the street—of memory and of historical re-creation; and, in imagination, join the unhurried audience at the entertainments to be found there. We can linger not only at the entertainers at whom we have paused in this brief saunter but at many, many others, like those itemised with such care by Mayhew, upon whose interviews we have already largely drawn: a dancing bear, performing dogs, a 'happy family' of birds, mice and a cat in one cage, glee singers, a poor harp player, a microscope and a telescope exhibitor, a street reciter, a sword swallower, a fire eater, a German band, the Chinese Shades, a whistling man . . .

Overleaf: 'Public Characters': detail from an aquatint by J. Gleadah after W. Heath, 1824

Above: Mechanical figures: early-nineteenth-century lithograph
Below: Jigging puppets: early-nineteenth-century lithograph

The Rainbow is perhaps the best remembered of all the classic coloured comics, and was the only comic known to be read by the royal children. The Brownie Boys were drawn by Albert Thacker Brown, Bertie to his contemporaries, but he was more at home in the penny *Butterfly* with his Smiler and Smudge. Secondary, but soon to be promoted, were the Bruin Boys, originated by Julius Stafford Baker.

Tuppenny Coloureds

BY DENIS GIFFORD

'PENNY PLAIN, Tuppence Coloured' meant one thing to Robert Louis Stevenson's generation, another thing to mine, yet the same thing to both. To them it meant sheets of cut-out characters for toy theatres, sold at a penny apiece, or hand-coloured for twopence. To us it meant sheets of characters, too, but our sheets came folded like tabloid newspapers, and our dramas were built in. No need to cut and paste and read lines aloud; our characters acted their succinct slapstickery behind the proscenia of panels. We were the inheritors of the New Literacy and our penny plains and tuppenny coloureds were 'the comics'.

Another parallel with Stevenson's sheets is the price bracket, so neatly dividing the rich from the poor. Penny comics were printed in black ink on paper that might be pink (*Chips*), green (*Butterfly*), or blue (*Jester*), and had eight pages. Tuppenny comics were printed in black, red, yellow and blue ink, on white paper, and had twelve pages. We children had a penny, never twopence, so *Chips* we bought for ourselves, *The Rainbow* was bought for us. And the publishers of the comics knew it. 'Buy next week's *Joker*, chums,' advised Arthur A. Wagg, the genial editor, 'and be sure of getting your Grand Free Potato Popgun!'; whereas Mrs Hippo, who, believe it or not, edited *Playbox*, would tactfully recommend asking Daddy to order next week's copy for a Grand Free Game of Coloured Quoits.

Because of this price and purchaser differential the character—and the characters—of the comics differed also. *Chips* and the other penny papers pictured a working-class world of comical policemen (Constable Cuddlecook, P.C. Penny the Bright Copper) and a workshy-class world of tramps (Weary Willie and Tired Tim, Willie Wart and Wally Warble). *The Rainbow* and its twopenny contemporaries portrayed middle-class families (The Jolly Adventures of Happy Harry and Sister Sue) and precocious pets (Dr Croc's Academy, Mrs Hippo's Boarding

School). There was an attention to literacy lamentably lacking
in the penn'orths. Office boys like Philpot Bottles of *Chips* might
address their readers as 'Deer foaks' and run 'Jeneral Nollidge'
tests with questions—sorry, 'kwestions'—like 'Who uttered the
faimuss larst werds, "Cor, stuff me up a plum tree, I'm sunk!"
Wos it Nelson, Charley Peece, Unkle Tom Cobbly, Dick Turnip,
Bud Flanagan, or me?' but the nearest Rupert the Chick was
allowed to illiteracy was his hyphenated 'Hal-lo! Hal-lo! Hal-lo!'
and his Mer-ry Rid-dle, 'Why is Mrs Quack-Quack like an
um-brel-la?' (Be-cause she has ribs. Ha! Ha!)

The pioneer of comics was Alexander Sloper, whose name in
contraction was the soubriquet for one who disappeared on the
eve of rent day. He was born in full grogblossom on Wednesday,
1 May 1867, in *Judy*, subtitled 'The London Serio-Comic Journal'.
Ally Sloper and his opposite number, the slippery Ikey Mo,
were the brain children of a prolific penman called Charles H.
Ross, who shortly took over editorship of that journal, shifting
the emphasis from Serio to Comic.

It was on Saturday, 3 May 1884, that this self-styled Friend of
Man finally came into his own with *Ally Sloper's Half-Holiday*,
an eight-page tabloid of cartoons and articles subtitled 'A Selec-
tion, Side-Splitting, Sentimental, and Serious, for the Benefit of
Old Boys, Young Boys, Odd Boys generally, and even Girls'.

The boom in comics began when young Alfred Harmsworth
launched his first ha'penny paper on 17 May 1890. *Comic Cuts'* initial
popularity is hard to understand. It was no different from any
of the well-established comics: its eight pages were packed with
reprinted cartoons and even reprinted text from *Answers*. Yet
within a year the circulation touched 300,000 a week.

Alfred Harmsworth's contributions to the popular press have
often been exaggerated, but one important milestone has been
curiously ignored, perhaps because in his nobler years Lord
Northcliffe considered his comic past undignified. On 29 August
1896 *Comic Cuts* appeared with the headline, 'An Interesting
Announcement Next Week'. Inside the editor followed this up:

I am preparing a special number of *Comic Cuts*, which is to be unlike any
number before produced, and unlike any paper ever before published in this

country. This may seem to boast and brag; but I am confident that when it goes out to the trade it will be an eye opener, and few people will believe it was printed in England. The printing trade will jump to the conclusion that it was printed in Paris. It will not be so. It will be the product of English labour, and may cause the biggest rush ever known in the history of the halfpenny paper trade.

The 'Coloured Autumn Number of the World-Famed Half-penny Comic Paper', went on sale on 12 September 1896, although printing problems caused it to be dated simply September. The front page bore a splash portrait captioned 'The man with a will who took a pink pill', and the back page ran a set of six pictures entitled 'The Elves and the Unspotted Egg' which involved a brushful of red paint, but otherwise the much vaunted 'Over Fifty Coloured Pictures' were simply tinted line drawings showing little use of colour.

SLOPER'S CHRISTMAS PUDDING.

"*Mamma's pudding, which has been on the make for the last month or six weeks, was duly inaugurated on Christmas Morning. Papa officiated, of course. The whole thing turned out a miserable failure, and the things which Pa had put into the pudding as a surprise, made most of us feel perfectly ill. Papa said he thought the Lucky Bag wheeze was a good one to perpetuate. Perhaps it is; but if this sort of horse-play goes on much longer, I shall leave home altogether and go on tour. Poor Papa seems to think that because everybody is talking about his 'Christmas Holidays' he can do what he likes.*"—Tootsie.

Adults Only: 'Ally Sloper' by W. F. Thomas,
Ally Sloper's Half-Holiday, 27 December 1890

This first British coloured comic, which was also the first British paper of any kind to be printed in four colours, had been printed for Harmsworth by the London Colour Printing Company 'at a rate of ten thousand an hour. Printing in four colours requires four times the amount of care and attention bestowed on the ordinary issue, and much longer time than usual.' *Wonder* and *Chips* tried an occasional foray into the field of polychromatic spectaculars, but it was an outsider who won the honour of publishing the first weekly coloured comic, calling it, with appropriate simplicity, *The Coloured Comic*.

Trapps and Holmes issued their number one on 21 May 1898. It was edited by a Mr C.C., who addressed his readers from 'The Editor's Colour box' thus: '*The Coloured Comic* has been a long thought-out project. It has necessitated the outlay of huge capital, so large indeed that I wonder where it all comes from. Sometimes I think it can be that the proprietors have been to the Klondyke and struck oil!' Mr C.C. could mix metaphors as well as colours, it seems, but he was certainly correct in predicting that his front page, the only one of the eight to be printed in full colour, would one day 'be worth at least ten times as much as the whole paper costs you.'

The Coloured Comic, albeit now printed in black on pink paper, was still a well-established weekly on 30 July 1904, the day Harmsworth issued number one of *Puck*, pronouncing it 'the first number of the first coloured comic paper'. His printers, the London Colour Printing Company, who had also produced the Trapps and Holmes comic, could have corrected him.

Up to this point in time the comics we have discussed conformed to the format of those we knew later, in the Golden Age of the 'thirties. Their content, however, was radically different. These primitive picture papers were all aimed at adults. What *Punch* was to the middle-aged middle-class and *Private Eye* is to the youthful dissenter, *Comic Cuts* and its fellows were to the working man. Proof of this can be found in their occasional publication of a story or set of pictures described editorially as 'Something for the Children'.

Puck was no different from the rest. Subtitled 'Jokes and Pictures for the Home', it modelled itself on the American Sunday supplements which by 1904 were being sold in this country. It not only ran strips reprinted from these newspaper sections, like George McManus's Newlyweds, but pirated such series as R. F. Outcault's Buster Brown under the name of Scorcher Smith. The first front page had been a superb strip detailing the Comic Adventures of Oliver Twist and the Artful Dodger, but this comic paper image was promptly eschewed for the following five months. Then, suddenly, an internal section for younger readers, called *Puck Junior*, was absorbed into the whole, and Johnny Jones arrived on the cover. In No. 22 he encountered the Casey Court Boys, a gang of ragamuffin refugees from *Chips*. *Puck* never looked back. Its days as a family magazine were done; we, the children, had taken over.

Puck, at a penny, was designed for the Johnny Joneses of the world, rather than the Billy Baggses; a world where daddy wore a topper, where mummy had the vicar to tea, where nursie walked out with a soldier boy, polly parrot nipped the tweenie, and cookie passed pies to her Robert. The artwork was splendid, clean and brightly coloured. Tom Wilkinson drew the back page experiments of Professor Radium the Scientific Man, and Jack B. Yeats, not yet a famous painter, drew Dr Up-to-date's Scientific Academy in a style far removed from his first work in the nineteenth-century *Comic Cuts*. He signed himself with a little bee. As the years passed, *Puck* changed very little. Artists came and went—A. B. Payne drew Tommy Traddles, then left to create Pip, Squeak and Wilfred for the *Daily Mirror*—but the bright surface remained placid, unbroken by a World War, undamaged by a General Strike. The Newlyweds, long abandoned by George McManus, metamorphosed into The Merry Mischiefs, with only Joey the Parrot left to tell the tale, and the greatest event in history according to *Puck* was the arrival of Rob the Rover.

This watershed in a mainstream of comedy was the first, and last, dramatic picture story in the comic's history. Rob, found adrift on a raft by dear old Dan, the grizzled fisherman, was still roving in search of an identity when the paper closed down twenty years later. Little did Walter Booth, hitherto a funny picture man, reck what was in store when he switched

'Rob the Rover' by Walter Booth, *Puck*, 24 October 1931

styles that fatal 15 May 1920. Booth's neat, careful drawing linked the comic strip with storybook illustration, and started the British school of picture-story technique. In time the whole comic went over to adventure strips, with many a wandering orphan in search of fame and fortune (Tom All-Alone, Little Miss Nobody), and a two-page spread in two colours, both by Booth, totalling twenty-four red-splashed panels: Captain Moonlight, a highwayman-cum-pirate adventure, and Rob, who had gone all science-fiction with one of those multi-purpose crafts called 'The Flying Fish'. Unexplained was Dan's sea-change from gnarled old fisherman to trim-bearded pilot of the future. Walter Booth died in Wales last February, eighty-three years old and unsung through being unsigned. But in a hundred dusty volumes and a million memories Rob roves ever on.

Meanwhile, in Red Lion Court, James Henderson, the publisher who had printed Alfred Harmsworth's first freelance pieces, saw his ex-contributor's colourful success with *Puck*. He out-Harmsworthed Harmsworth by producing *Lot-O'-Fun* in full colour for a ha'penny! True, it had but eight pages to *Puck*'s twelve, but half of them were in colour. The back page, in blue and yellow panels, presented Dreamy Daniel. George Davey drew the dream-life of this tattered tramp, whose unlikely encounters with anything and anybody, from fairy queens to

Fatty Arbuckle, soon moved to the full-colour front page where he stayed for twenty years or more.

Lot-O'-Fun's success led Henderson to add colour to his *Comic Life*, which had started as *Pictorial Comic Life* in 1898. Both papers were fond of featuring cut-out models, which is why they are rare today. This popular feature was the first thing to go when Henderson finally threw in the towel; *Lot-O'-Fun* No. 731, 13 March 1920, bore the changed imprint, 'Published by the proprietors, the Amalgamated Press Ltd, Fleetway House, Farringdon Street'. Our old pal Dreamy Daniel was cut down, but remained to share the coloured cover with an interesting innovation, a large dramatic illustration from one of the interior serials, drawn by an artist called, oddly enough, Daniel. The unknown experts who laid the Ben Day tints for the London Colour Printing Company had worked wonders in the six-picture strips; now they had a field day. The range of effects they achieved for the series called Tomba of the Gorillas is striking, especially in this modern day of mechanical colour.

Chuckles was Harmsworth's first halfpenny coloured comic, launched on 10 January 1914 as his reply to the Henderson twins. Breezy Ben and Dismal Dutchy made a colourful couple on

'The Golden Arrow' by Reg Perrott, *Puck*, 25 June 1938

the cover, but inside Mustard Keen and his Terrible Terrier and Boxo the Muscular Marvel were but black on white.

The first *Rainbow* shone forth on 14 February 1914, but its cover stars, the Bruin Boys, were already old hands at making mischief. Arthur Mee had persuaded Alfred Harmsworth to publish a monthly educational part-work for young readers, under Mee's editorship. *The New Children's Encyclopaedia* was launched, complete with a Grand Free Cinema, on 15 February 1910. Wisely, Mee leavened his instruction with laughter. Inside this sevenpenny magazine was an eight-page section called *The Playhour*, with four pages in full colour. Two of the pages were devoted to a strip called Frolic Farm. The artist was J. S. Baker, who was already drawing Casey Court in *Chips*. Baker liked drawing funny animals; indeed his street urchins looked like monkeys. In the fourth instalment of the encyclopaedia the fun section was rechristened *The Playbox* and Baker's strip became Mrs Hippo's Boys. It was subtitled 'How Tiger Tim and Jacko Provided a Fine Feast.' Two years later *The Playbox* was so popular it was made into a Christmas Annual, the first of its kind to be published by the Amalgamated Press. The stars were Tiger Tim and the Bruin Boys—Georgie Giraffe, Joey the parrot, Jumbo the elephant, Fido the pup, Jacko the monkey, Willie the ostrich, and Bobby Bruin. Porkyboy, that greedy bane of Mrs Bruin's Boarding School, was not introduced until some time after Harry Foxwell, the best of the Tiger Tim artists, took over *The Rainbow* front page in the twenties. When Foxwell was lured to the *Daily Mail* to take on the Teddy Tail comic supplement in 1933, a lot of the life left Tim & Co, but soon Bert Wymer settled in to make over the Bruin Boys in his own careful mould and produce some of the most colourful covers the comic had ever seen. *Tiger Tim's Weekly* began in 1920 as a two-colour job, but soon burst into full flaming four. Despite personal management by Tim himself ('Carry your *Weekly* at the seaside, and if the *Tiger Tim* man sees you with it he will present you with a lovely coloured balloon!') and an eternity of unending adventure with Pat the Pirate, it merged with *The Rainbow* after twenty years!

Playtime was the pioneer in that half-size field, later exploited so successfully by the D. C. Thomson group (*Dandy, Beano, Magic,*

Glamour girl: 'Susie Sunshine and her Pretty Pet
Poms' by Anton Lock, *The Rainbow*, 30 January 1915

Sparky). Its star artist was a star indeed, Harry Rountree. This
Aucklander specialised in animal life, and his four-colour
covers, using one big picture in what would later become the
American comic-book format, are exceptional by any comic-
paper standard. He drew a centre-spread strip, too, Coral Island,
or Jill and her Jungle Friends, and in this introduced, years
before Disney, a little character called Micky Mouse. *Playtime*
began as a magazine, but soon went the way of all success by
adding comic sets in red and black. Ultimately it succumbed to
standardisation by expanding to full tabloid size, with Teddy and
Tilda and Mrs Whiskers' Scamps on page one and Robin Hood's
Revenge on page twelve, before Uncle Dan announced that as
from next week he was changing the name to *Bo-Peep*! *Playtime*
had been the first new coloured comic published since the
14–18 war had curtailed comics in both circulation and size.
It lasted from 29 March 1919 to 12 October 1929, twenty times the
run of the A.P.'s second post-war venture, *The Sunday Fairy*. This
experiment in uplift started on 10 May 1919, but by October had
turned title to *The Children's Fairy*. Decorative but doomed, this
pretty comic finally burst into *Bubbles* on 16 April 1921, settling
down for a solid score of years. Foxwell had the front page where,
as a change from a board school full of assorted animals, he

drew a board school full of assorted boys. And a colourful crew they were: Jackie, a bob-haired British blond, Ching the yellow chinky-boy, Snowball the fur-clad Eskimo, Hans the happy Dutchie, Redwing the feathered redskin, and Pompey the inky 'nig', supervised, if that is the word, by mob-capped Mrs Bunty, who frequently held her hands high with the cry, 'What is the meaning of this?', in the approved Mrs Bruin manner.

A more successful experiment was *Chicks' Own*, which mixed education and entertainment by splitting its syllables. Dating from 25 September 1920, the fluffy front-page Rupert the Chick grew not one pinfeather in all his thirty-seven-year career. Even in 1957, when the comic joined forces with the gravure *Playhour*, Rupert's black chum was known as Nig-ger. Big, bright pictures were the order of the editor, who had a predilection for calling everything a Tale: Pot and Pan Tales, Pig Tales, Pussy Cat Tales, Teddy Tales, and, of course, Tales of Ned-dy and Nel-lie Nig-ger. The success of the comic with parents who wanted their children to learn to read prompted the A.P. to produce a partner, and *Tiny Tots* was born in all its hyphenated glory on 22 October 1927. Tiny and Tot bedevilled their pretty Nursie for thirty-two years, surely a record for loyal service.

The Sunbeam was next to shine, from 7 October 1922, and was

Hy-phen-a-ted Dra-ma: 'Lit-tle Snow-drop'
by Frank Jennens, *Tiny Tots*, 3 May 1930

only blacked out by the last war. At first it featured Fun in Funny Folks Forest and Mrs Blossom and her Little Blossoms, but in later years it went in for picture stories, with the Merry Adventures of Molly and Mick, Dick and Doris, Detectives, and Carrots—the Story of a London Waif. Molly and Mick mixed serialised escapades with comic paper comedy, as they eluded the yellow clutches of Li-Lo the Pirate on Oogli-Woogli Island, to cries of 'Here we are again' from Percy the Parrot.

On 14 February 1925 appeared the first comic produced exclusively for girls. *Playbox* played safe by unveiling on page one the hitherto unsuspected secret that the Bruin Boys had a complete set of identical twin sisters! These were the Hippo Girls; Mrs Bruin, it seems, was unique. There were Tiger Tilly, Gertie Giraffe, Pearl Porky, Betty Bear, Polly Parrot, Jenny Jacko, and Baby Jumbo. Occasionally a female ostrich could be seen craning around the corner, but her name seems never to have been revealed. Harry Foxwell drew this crew as though they were the Bruin Boys in drag. But the hoped-for female appeal failed, and Mrs Hippo removed her Boarding School to the back page.

Sparkler started on 20 October 1934. Penny comic men turned up with cartoons in colour: Bertie Brown, creator of Constable Cuddlecook and the Capers of Charlie Chaplin, drew the cover, Kitty and Ken and Koko the Comical Coon, and 'Charley' Pease converted his Casey Court to Freddy Flicker and his Film Fans.

Suddenly, on 8 February 1936, the mighty Amalgamated Press woke up to find they no longer had the corner in coloured comics. Odhams Press had joined forces with Walt Disney Productions to publish the first full-colour photogravure comic: 'Here it is at last—no, not the elephant's tail, but the Very First Issue of my Very Own Weekly Paper! And it's what the fire-irons called the kitchen range, isn't it . . . just grate!' So the legendary Mickey Mouse greeted his Chums in number one of *Mickey Mouse Weekly*. The cover, a blaze of colour and corn ('Hey, Horace, I'm a born musician—I've even got drums in my ears!'), was painted by Haughton, who had been drawing the *Mickey Mouse Annual* for Deans. The rest was a mixture of hand-coloured daily and Sunday strips syndicated from America, and original English artwork. Basil Reynolds, who would ultimately flower into a brilliant natural history artist, slapped out Skit and Skat (the World's Smallest Cabin Boy and his Skatty Cat), and H. Stanley White, hitherto a historical strip man in *Bo-Peep*, rocketed into the future with a science-fiction saga, Ian on Mu.

The A.P.'s answer to Mickey Mouse was *Happy Days*. It was the last coloured comic to be launched before the 1939 war, and the finest of them all. Deliberately designed as a quality comic, beautifully coloured in full photogravure, and drawn by the best artists in Fleetway House, it marked the apogee of achievement in the British comic and ended the Golden Age in a blaze of glory. I still recall the delight of that day, 8 October 1938, when I clapped my dazzled eye on number one. My favourite cartoonist, Roy Wilson, scooped the cover with Chimpo's Circus, and his splendid drawings, so great in the old penny blacks, shone in Sun Engraving splendour. The centre spread had two picture serials: Wonder Island used colour strikingly, whilst Sons of the Sword proved that young Reg Perrott would certainly have become our leading straight strip man had he lived. But the *Happy Days* were short ones. 1939 dawned, and as dark clouds gathered in that innocent skyful of sunbeams and rainbows, I felt my first touch of impending doom. One day I went to buy my *Happy Days* and was handed a shabby imitation, a pale thing of run-of-the-mill rotary-press colouring instead of gravure delight. A few weeks later, in issue number 45, the editor had some advice for me. Next week, he suggested, I should ask for *Chicks' Own*. What an end for an eleven-year-old's favourite comic! I did not take the editor's advice and within a month I was an evacuee. I don't know which hurt more.

And that is really the end. Except that you may have been wondering about the answer to Philpot Bottles' Jeneral Nollidge kwestion. The faimuss larst werds were, in fact, uttered by Bottles himself—'When my canew skuttled itself in the tiddler pond last Saterday!'

All the illustrations are from comics in Denis Gifford's collection, and for permission to reproduce them grateful acknowledgement is made to I.P.C. Magazines, Ltd. and, in the case of *Mickey Mouse Weekly*, to Walt Disney Productions, Ltd.

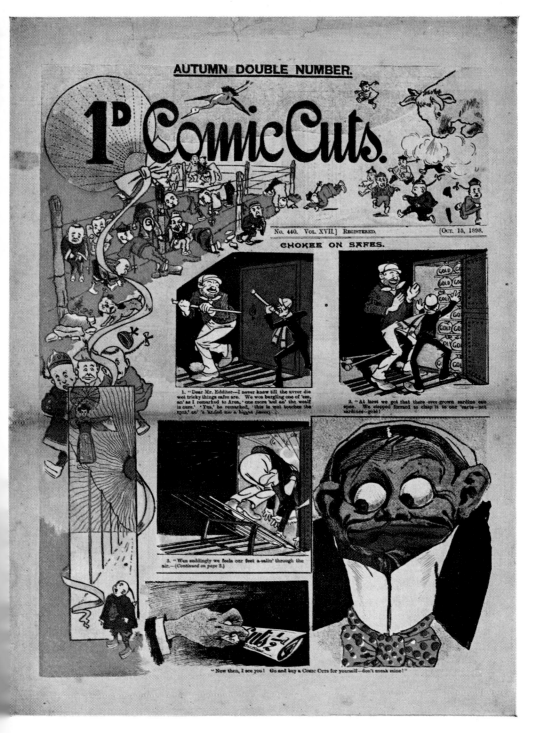

Comic Cuts was the original 'ha'penny black'; it was also the original coloured comic, bursting into double-sized, double-priced, and quadruple-coloured numbers. Front-page stars are Chokee Bill and Area Sneaker, typical anti-heroes of the period, sharing space with that obligatory character for colour editions, a Negro.

Chuckles was Harmsworth's first halfpenny coloured comic, produced in answer to Henderson's *Comic Life* and *Lot-o'-Fun*. Tom Wilkinson, one of the early masters, drew this fine front page when the First World War was five months old, yet his nautical hero, Breezy Ben, seems not to have answered Kitchener's call.

Puck was the first of Harmsworth's coloured comics, though not the first coloured comic, as he claimed. It began as a cartoon magazine for adults, but soon the inside section called *Puck Junior* took over. Angel and her Merry Playmates are here drawn by the late Walter Booth, better remembered for his pioneering picture serial 'Rob the Rover'.

Lot-o'-Fun, originally a Henderson publication, shortly after its takeover by the Amalgamated Press, showing Dreamy Daniel's displacement by Tomba of the Gorillas. Daniel was drawn by George Davey and Tomba was drawn by Daniel. The latter artist was no sloth, as can be seen by his imaginative use of mechanical tints. Pitch and Toss the Nautical Nuts made their debut in page five.

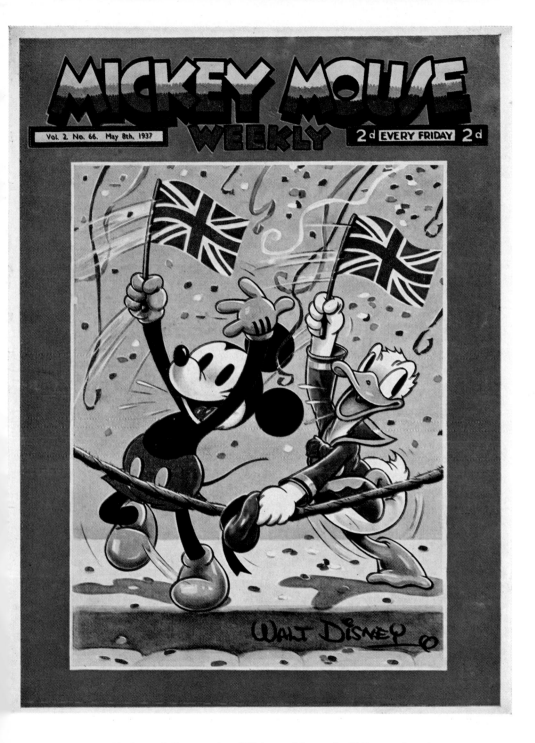

Mickey Mouse Weekly Special Coronation Edition with, as the Editor pointed out on page two, a cover 'specially drawn for all of you by Mr Disney, and as you see, it bears his own signature. Be sure and cut it out and frame it', he added, ensuring the rarity of the complete comic for future collectors. The comments of Mr Haughton, who usually drew the comic's cover, are not recorded.

Tiger Tim's Weekly shows the famous Bruin Boys getting ready for the impending Yule. The artist is Herbert Foxwell, soon to take over Teddy Tail for the *Daily Mail*. The Bumpty Boys, triplets so inseparable they might have been Siamese, were drawn by Frederick Crompton. The centre spread in black and red featured Wonderful Tales of Tinkle-Bell Tree and Pinkie and Patsy of Pat-a-Cake Palace.

Happy Days, the Amalgamated Press's answer to Odhams' *Mickey Mouse Weekly*, was a costly flop. Its use of full-colour photogravure was years ahead of its time, and produced some delightful effects. The front page was drawn by the late Roy Wilson, best of all the penny comic men. He drew some fine fronts for *Tip Top* when that penny paper went into colour during the last war.

Making Them Laugh

BY PAUL JENNINGS

I T IS A DREADFUL confession for a writer to have to make,
but when you call to mind any great comedian you do not
think first of jokes he made, of songs he sang, of words at all.
Obviously these follow—marvellous, utterly characteristic words
truly inseparable from your memory of the man, of the sound
of his voice. But the first impression is not even visual either.
It is of a presence, a spirit, a man: a man standing up there (or,
if these are early memories and you were still up in 'the gods',
down there) able to do something both to you personally and to
everyone else.

He is able to make a mysterious communication with the audience—that tiger; to make it lie down and be tickled, helplessly,
asking for more. Up to now it will have been outside things:
watching the acrobats, the one-man band, the dancers, from
outside. But now, if the comedian is of the pure metal, there
will be something quite different from the yawn described by
Macneice:—

> Where pink thighs flash like the spokes of a wheel, where we feel
> That we know in advance all the jogtrot and the cakewalk jokes,
> All the bumfun and the gags of the comedians in boaters and toques.

Like all great artists, the great comedian can make all other
considerations—your past, your personal life, your worries and
hopes, the whole fabric of life and cities, the entire outside
world—vanish into unreality. Just for this timeless moment of
laughter you are in—ah, not just *his* world, that's the beauty
of it—you are in a shared paradise, almost in that state of lost
innocence, before the mere adult intellect stepped in, where
the laughter of happiness is the same thing as the laughter of
humour. He may *begin* with this (as it were) secondary laughter
of humour, but as the act proceeds that kind of self-conscious
'appreciation' of individual jokes gives way to a kind of general-
ised happiness on an altogether higher plane. In just the same

The Old Bedford Music Hall
Painting by W. R. Sickert, c. 1890
(Fitzwilliam Museum, Cambridge)

way, now and again at a concert the real thing happens; it is no longer a matter of appreciating particular turns of phrase but of actually living in the music, *being* it. So with laughter.

To be traitorous for just one more paragraph to the sacred cause of words and articulation, I can think of several occasions when I have entered, or rather been brought into, this magic world of total, helpless laughter by purely visual means. There were the two clowns in Bertram Mills's circus before the war who, with a step ladder and some hundred buckets of water, provided a delirious ten minutes simply because each had the transparent design of pouring a bucket into the trousers of the other. There was the sublime scene in *Duck Soup* where Groucho, aware that Chico and Harpo were made up to resemble him exactly, performed a wonderful pantomime, all the time attempting to find out if the figure reflecting him was a real person or a real reflection. There was that wonderful troupe of acrobats, with doleful Edwardian moustaches and long thin shorts, who filled the stage of the Palladium with endless preparation and cries of 'Hup!' and never actually *did* anything. . . .

But of course it is words that give the thing its final completion, its total humanity. Much as I admire the greatest mime in the world, Marcel Marceau, after twenty minutes I get tired of his arbitrary silence; I want to hear him speak. I can't picture those clowns doing anything *else* but pour water; and God knows Groucho never kept quiet for long.

All the great stand-up comics stood up and *spoke*. And they spoke their own words, not those of script-writers. Their words were a perfection, an extension of themselves. If there was collaboration it was with a partner, not a writer. I remember Murray and Mooney, for instance. Murray (or it may have been Mooney) would attempt a long dramatic story or poem, which Mooney (or Murray), sucking a fag-end mysteriously as alight at the end of the act as at the beginning, would constantly interrupt:

"Ere, do you know, when I was born, I weighed one pound, one ounce.'
'Did you? And did you live?'
'Did I live! You should see me now.'

Two more lines of recitation, then:

''Ere, do you know, I 'ave found a way to catch fish without any bait.'
'Well, how do you catch fish without any bait?'
'I have a calendar, an alarm clock, and a lawn-mower. I go down to the river an' I set orf the alarm clock, an' it wakes the fish up, an' they come up to look at the calendar to see what day it is, an' then I cut orf their 'eads with the lawn-mower.'

There was a thin, not altogether distinguishable line between the self-spoken words of these great men and actual ad-libbing. Certainly it sounded like ad-libbing, although doubtless it was the well-rehearsed spontaneity practised by speakers in more serious spheres, such as Winston Churchill, trying out his gestures and quips before a mirror.

There are comics about today who retain the technique of inspired ad-libbing; one thinks instantly of Ted Ray and Tommy Trinder. But these are men who learnt in the days when there were music halls all over the country in which to practise their art (and as a curious side-note to this, many of the last—and sometimes I think mournfully it is *the* last—generation of post-war comics graduated not from music hall but the Windmill Theatre in London. Harry Secombe, Jimmy Edwards, Tony Hancock, John Tilley, Eric Barker and others must have sharpened their wit on some of the dreariest audiences in the world; whatever they came for—what am I saying, we *know* what they came for—it wasn't laughter, so if you could make *them* laugh you could make anybody laugh).

Getting the bird on TV is such a time-delayed and confusing process, with so many other people—producers, cameramen, script-writers—involved, that the comic can't possibly learn the direct lessons from it which he absorbed the night they threw tomatoes in Burnley. In the true performance there has to be this underlying possibility of failure, this feeling that *now* is a unique occasion, for the great triumph, the great resounding wave of continuing laughter, to be possible.

It is significant that one of the best ways for a young unknown comic to get known today is to include in his act impressions of better-known showbiz people. It's as though audiences, distrusting the whole idea of comedy anyway, and not quite sure by what standards to judge the man before them, had said to themselves: 'At least we know what Sammy Davis or Mick Jagger are like; now we can see if this chap's any good or not.'

In the days of the great stand-up comic it was the other way round. He had an audience of whom it could be assumed that, a comic idea once having been planted, they would want to sit back and watch it unfold. I know it was a film and not music-hall, but that mirror sequence from *Duck Soup* illustrates my point. Once the Marxes had set up the idea that Groucho wasn't sure whether he was facing his own reflection or another actual man, the variations followed as logically as in Euclid.

Harry Tate went about the country with his motoring sketch practically unchanged for thirty years. Nobody wanted him to change it. The more it was the same the more polished it became, the more its audiences savoured delicious inevit-ability; laughter can be more intense when you know what's coming.

Because of this, the great stand-up comics could be super-latively themselves. They didn't need script-writers or situation comedy. A man like Sid Field *was* a situation in himself. And I don't think the art declined through any inner weakness but because of radio and TV, especially the latter (for radio was a fertile soil for characters like Handley or Edwards, even though they also inaugurated the script-writer era). TV, now they've invented Ampex tape, likes to have everything cut-and-dried. And the only counter to such predictability is surrealism.

Ultimately audiences, and even their TV equivalents, for which I think it is time the word *vidences* was coined, will tire of the instant-joke act of one-line gags *and* the situation comedy and will find they hunger for something more sustaining; more human, in fact. The brilliant, unexpected, surrealist surprise is fine, but a half-hour programme of a succession of such instant jokes becomes wearying. And in nine out of ten situation comed-ies you can hear the gears grinding.

So where will they go for it? Well, the only place I can go to is Clacton Pier (where I've seen two unknowns who subsequently achieved national fame). But that'll be the day, when they hope to get on TV as a prelude to Clacton Pier! Or the Ipswich Hippo-drome, or the Aston Hippodrome. Or the *London* Hippodrome.

Except for the pictures of Sid Field and W. C. Fields, the photographs which follow are from the Mander & Mitchenson Collection.

Harry Tate, with his son Ronald, in his 'Motoring' sketch

58

Every line in the body of George Robey (Commander of the British Empire, and eventually Sir) recalls an age when comics didn't have to hurry through a succession of one-line cracks. The personality flowered in his language: 'Kindly temper your hilarity with a modicum of decorum.' He was a character comedian—and the character, whether vicar, bridesmaid or pantomime Dame, always had a red nose, addressed the audience in a hoarse conspiratorial whisper with 'honest vulgarity', and was always George Robey.

Like many great comics, Billy Bennett was one who let the audience do all the smiling. ' 'Twas a dirty night, and a dirty trick, when our ship turned turtle in the At-lan-tic'; and, after a ponderous pause, 'Well, it *rhymes*.' He was billed as 'Almost a Gentleman' and all his parodies and monologues were interlaced with marvellously would-be cultured asides, or perhaps a few indescribably serious ballet steps. His fame, between the wars, coincided with the last phase of uneroded music-hall glory.

Will Hay was an amateur astronomer, but his schoolmaster sketches did not exactly give the impression of a giant intellect among pygmies; indeed there seemed little to choose between him and the Old Man (Moore Marriott) and the Fat Boy (Graham Moffatt) who often appeared with him in unlikely institutions besides schools, such as police or fire stations (also seen in memorable films). He was superb at puzzlement, deadpan and double-take. 'You boys gambling?' 'Yessir.' 'For money?' 'Yessir. Want a hand?' 'What, ME? Gamble?' Pause. 'Orright.' He was Nature's, as well as the casting director's, choice for the part of Dr Smart-Aleck in the film about Beachcomber's famous school, Narkover.

Monsewer Eddie Gray in a rare attitude—smiling. For quite a lot of his act he would mutter gloomily as he juggled brilliantly, occasionally hurling into the wings one of the objects being juggled with. Sometimes he would start with an impenetrable, involved card trick, introduced for some reason in pidgin French—'I cuttee the cards, vang-seess ici, vang-seess there-see.' Then he would abandon the whole thing for juggling ('this is the trick I usually broadcast'), later suddenly yelling *Ten of diamonds!'* He joined the Crazy Gang, often as one who interrupted their act from a box. 'I happen to be the Norwegian Ambassador. You have just insulted my country.' This when the others were clearly in Greek costume. 'But this is Greek.' 'Oh.' And he would sit down again, though not for long. The funniest man in the world.

Sid Field was the brightest of the post-war comic stars, perhaps the last true genius of the music hall. One view is that there have been three great clowns in 150 years; Grimaldi, Dan Leno, Sid Field. His death in 1950, aged forty-five, was a tragedy. He had the supreme gift of being able to imply that he himself knew the absurdity of a situation even while he played it with total conviction. In his famous golfing sketch, when Jerry Desmonde, as the professional, instructed him to 'get behind the ball' he replied with unanswerable, lunatic logic: 'But it's behind all round it.' As a soccer fan he would yell hoarsely: 'Use your own judgment!' As J. C. Trewin said, 'his humour was the gold of the spirit.'

63

W. C. Fields is best known in England for his famous film performance as Mr Micawber; but the dyspeptic, child-hating ('Your line is *goo goo*; don't muff it'), alcoholic ('There is no such thing as a large whisky') character seemed to spill over from his vaudeville and film career into real life. It is said that, obsessed by the fear of dying in poverty, he opened bank accounts in many towns where he was playing, under such names as Mahatma Kane Jeeves, Cuthbert J. Twillie, Otis Criblecolis and Egbert Sousé. Some of his remarks ('I'd rather have two girls at twenty-one each than one girl at forty-two') have become folk-sayings, notably: 'It ain't a fit night out for man or beast.'

Douglas Byng is not strictly speaking a music-hall comic, although as a *grande dame* of Dames he has appeared in pantomime. Cabaret and revue have been his forte, providing him with the right kind of audience to savour his appearance as 'Doris, the Goddess of Wind', 'Millie, a messy old Mermaid', or as a castle, complete with strategically placed drawbridge. He designs these costumes himself. A master—or maybe mistress —of *double entente*.

There are, of course, plenty of female names in the history of music hall or vaudeville, though most of them belonged to women who were primarily singers. But nobody would deny that Nellie Wallace was a mistress of music-hall comedy, a male-dominated field. Billed as 'The Essence of Eccentricity', wearing multi-coloured socks, elastic-sided boots, a stringy boa, and always a hat topped by a nodding feather, she would project in a quavering but everywhere audible voice such songs as 'Next Sunday morning is our Wedding Day'.

66

Tommy Trinder, lantern-jawed, knowing, quick Cockney wit, came up the hard way: working-men's clubs in the early 'twenties, music hall, concert party at Shanklin. At one time he was doing, every day, two shows at Finsbury Park Empire, three at the State, Kilburn, two at the Holborn Empire, and a night-club stint at the Paradise Club; and he said to his agent, 'I don't seem to be doing anything in the mornings.' He is known as a brilliant ad-libber, not from an instant mental card-index of jokes, like some, but from real creative flashes, although his act is often peppered with prepared asides; e.g., as late-comer arrives in dinner jacket, 'Sorry, sir, we had to start without you. Trouble with the bike?'

67

It is not only Jimmy Durante's nose but his entire personality that seems larger than life. Quite as many stories are told of his off-stage life as of his lines in a long career in vaudeville and films. Almost everyone knows the one about his being woken before dawn by his week-end host to go shooting, and trailing behind the others slapping each tree as he passed it. Asked why, he said: 'While I'm awake, no boid's gonna sleep.' It is said that when he buys such things as shirts he buys six and gives the other five away. Interviewed after being guest of honour at a banquet, he said: 'Well, foist of all we had the *pâté de foie gras.*' 'Could you tell the listeners what that is, Jimmy?' 'Whaddya mean? It's enough I can say it!'

Norman Wisdom has perhaps suffered from perfecting a very good music-hall technique. By the time he arrived at Collins' Music Hall in 1945, after appearance in war-time concert parties, the sun was beginning to set on music hall, and some critics have tended to go on as though his acrobatic abilities were his only ones. But, even though not everyone can fall down as skilfully as he does, there have always been inspired moments in his films when it is clear that no one else can do what he does when he gets up either, e.g. as humble worker answering phone in manager's office, drawn into delirious posh impersonation.

'I've got a Fireman's song, sir, with a real fireman's helmet.' Hostile manager from wings: 'It looks like it's been in a real fire.' Horace Kenney was an absolute original. Lugubrious to the point of genius, he was the supreme master of the straight, not to say acutely miserable, face. 'I went to visit a friend in the 'orspital. I read 'im the railway timetable all the way from Gravesend to Bury St Edmunds to cheer 'im up.' His mournfulness was increased by evident fear of the manager. 'Well, sir, I've got the Jolly Laughing Cobbler's Song. . . . "I laugh ha ha, I laugh hee hee"—No, I said "ha ha" when I should have said "hee hee" . . .'

Max Miller, the quintessential Cockney 'Cheeky Chappie', was not the diminutive that these words might suggest. He was a very large man, in even larger, outlandish suits, with big blue eyes perpetually surprised at the audience thinking 'filthy things'. In a non-stop rattle of patter he would run on past the point of the gag, then stop in surprise at the laughter. ' 'Ere's another thing: feller took 'is wife to Paris—there's a novelty to begin with, like taking coals to Newcastle. . . .' Or he would come on with a black eye—'How should I know there was a door handle *inside* the wardrobe?'

71

Frankie Howerd has the air of a perpetually surprised horse, and in addition
to variety, radio, TV and pantomime has appeared in Shakespeare, notably
as a memorable Bottom and as Launcelot Gobbo. He brings his own style
of pregnant pauses and heavy asides to the audience about 'them'. This
can refer either to the management or the rest of the cast, and as he often
appears in somewhat outrageous shows like the Folies Bergère or *Up Pompeii*,
the field is wide and there are profound depths of innuendo.

Fairground Baroque

BY OLIVE COOK

PHOTOGRAPHS BY EDWIN SMITH

THE SPECIAL SMELL, the unique sound, the stupendous imagery of the Fair must be among the most sharply remembered experiences of anyone whose childhood belongs to the years before the outbreak of the Second World War. The smell was the unforgettable smell of steam and hot brass; the sound was the blare of the mechanical organ; the imagery was that of the gargantuan scrolls, curves and swags, the moving statues, the flaring-nostrilled, bold-eyed horses and monsters of the round-abouts and side-shows. The photographs reproduced here recall the excitement of that experience and the flavour of the period prior to the advent of diesel power and the panatrope, of pop music and candy-floss, when the traction engine was the work-horse of the fairground.

My concern here is not with the history of the Fair itself, with its medieval origins and its metamorphosis from a trade centre to a tremendous entertainment, but with the influences which may have shaped the peculiar, predominating visual idiom of the traditional merry-go-round, booth and caravan. All the evidence suggests that this flamboyant expression of popular taste was a late development. Jules Bloch in a study of the gipsies and other 'travelling people' describes the richly carved and painted caravan as a nineteenth-century innovation and adds, significantly, that this form of dwelling was seldom preferred by the true gipsy, but was adopted by jugglers, tumblers, mountebanks and showmen. Again, early pictures of fairgrounds give no hint of the exuberance, glitter and brilliance we associate with them. In Hogarth's engraving of Southwark Fair all the animation derives from the figures: a performer on a slack-rope, a man flying from a tower to the ground by means of a groove fastened to his breast, a showily dressed woman beating the drum, a Negro trumpeter, a performing dog. The booths are remarkably plain except for a series of show-cloths—paintings on canvas hung from poles to advertise the various entertainments. In a coloured acquatint of 1808 by Rowlandson and Pugin the side-shows of Bartholomew Fair are conspicuously raised on high platforms and one of them is illuminated by gaudy lanterns and embellished with a scalloped fascia board, while another is covered with rectangular panels of diverse sizes exhibiting animal paintings, but there is no trace of Baroque ornament, and the lettering remains as sober as that on a Georgian shop front. Swing boats and a merry-go-round make their appearance in this picture, but they too are of basic severity. The merry-go-round consists of a narrow platform turned by hand, the swing boats of unadorned wooden crescents. Even in Cruikshank's impressions of Bartholomew Fair, where the fronts of the side-shows have assumed the guise of stage prosceniums, pediments and columns are informed by Palladian regularity and the decoration, confined to chaste lettering and roundels, flower garlands and the Royal Arms, is no more than a pallid reflection of that of the actual theatre.

The line of descent of much of the painted, as distinct from the carved, imagery of the fairground is clear. The pictures adorning the boxing booth, shown on page 82, the depictions of the lady defying death and the buck-jumping horse and Buffalo Bill cowboy next to it, the wholly captivating representations of the Indescribable Girl on the same page and the array of wild animals, part of a tremendous hunt, on the revolving rim of the great wheel of shafts of the subject of the opening photograph, are all of the same primitive genre as those paintings which appear in Hogarth's 'Southwark Fair'. The connection is yet more emphatically demonstrated if these roundabout decorations are compared with the show-cloths figuring in yet another eighteenth-century picture, 'A Village Fair' by Joseph Parry, reproduced in M. Wilson Disher's *Fairs, Circuses and Music Halls*. The booths in this canvas are hung with a painting of a contortionist and with six delineations of wild beasts directly related to those enlivening the merry-go-round.

The prototypes of the paintings of romantic landscapes which sometimes fill the panels of fairground structures, are also to be sought in earlier manifestations of the travelling show. Such landscapes occurred among the scenes exhibited in the large peep-shows which were a popular attraction of the Fair during the eighteenth and nineteenth centuries. The pictures were invariably interspersed with dramatic views of such subjects as a volcano in eruption, a castle on a moonlit rock, or a ruin looming through mist. But of the setting which gives all such paintings their particular character in the later fairground, the heavy, convoluted frames, the gorgeous friezes and the elaborately twirled and shaded lettering, there is no trace before the very end of the nineteenth century. We do indeed read of a handsomely gilded and painted horse in the advertisement for a spectacle presented at Bartholomew Fair in 1707 by a showwoman called Mrs Mynn; and the same spectacle, *The Trojan Horse*, included a Temple of Diana with 'capitals, urns, crescents, festoons and other carved work, all gilt and ten statues of the heathen gods, all gilt'. But we can only guess at the style of the decoration. If the Trojan horse at all resembled the painted animal announcing this very entertainment in Hogarth's 'Southwark Fair' it was decidedly naturalistic and bore no family likeness to the roundabout gallopers so vividly patterned with coarsely carved foliage, flowers and volutes. These exotic creatures seem to have come into being only when the steam engine had revolutionised the hand-turned merry-go-round.

The steam-driven roundabout was first evolved by a country blacksmith and wheelwright, Frederick Savage of King's Lynn, as a sideline to his work on agricultural machinery. The steam engine generated the power that set the coloured lights of the fairground so insistently aglow, churned forth the 'Poet and Peasant' or 'Zampa' overtures from the slotted cardboard of the organ, and sent the wooden horses charging through the magic forest of twisting brass rods. The alliance of steam engine and organ was immediately responsible for the magnificent visual character of the Fair at its peak in the Edwardian period. For the splendid key-frame 'paper' organ (so-called because of its perforated tune sheet) could never have taken the place of the former barrel organ on the fairground without the accompaniment of steam power; and the key-frame organ is the most likely source of fairground Baroque.

The names of the mechanical-organ makers are commemorated on such of their products as still survive in private collections and in the possession of the few showmen who continue to travel with traditional, old-style entertainments (no more than seventeen in 1966). The most important of these manufacturers were Gavioli, Marenghi, Mortier, Schiappa, Varetta, Limonaire, Ruth and Bruder; and family and business links eventually connected them all. Marenghi started his career in the Gavioli firm; Schiappa and Varetta were closely involved with Gavioli; Mortier and Gavioli combined; Limonaire, Ruth and Bruder were all associated with Gavioli; and even the Berni Organ Company of New York imported their organs from Gavioli, Ruth and Bruder. The Gavioli family were the most celebrated of these organ makers. They came originally from Modena and their history begins with the granting of a patent in 1855 to Lodovico Gavioli, Professor of Mechanics, for a portable reed organ. From the 'eighties the family, who had migrated to Paris in about 1876 and had become Gavioli et Compagnie, concentrated on the evolution of the paper organ. The first patent for a fully developed mechanism of this kind was granted to Anselme Gavioli in 1895. Very shortly afterwards Adolf Ruth, a member of a Black Forest firm who had specialised in barrel organs since 1842, built a paper-operated organ which played Weber's Jubilee Overture. Ruth and the Bruder family, who were making organs in the same town of Waldkirch, were affiliated both with Gavioli and Limonaire.

In view of these ramifications it is not surprising that the design of organ fronts and the array of figures on them, conductors, musicians and dancers, no matter whether they appeared beneath the name of Gavioli, Marenghi, Ruth, Bruder or Limonaire, should reveal a strong family likeness. Many of them indeed were actually by the same hand, that of the Bavarian sculptor Josef Dopp. And what more probable than that Dopp should have based his designs on the great explosive art in his immediate neighbourhood, on the fabulous exteriors and stucco interiors of the Baroque churches and palaces of

Continued on page 85

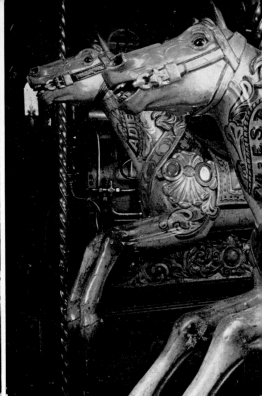

Fairground sculpture at its Edwardian peak. The traditional gallopers have been joined by creatures deriving from the wildest excesses of Baroque imagery. The style was set by the Bavarian designer of the first key-frame organ cases.

The name of the most celebrated mechanical organ maker, Gavioli, appears above the array of pipes, the visual impact of which echoes that of the coconut

saloon. The lettering behind the show-woman reveals a unique fairground custom, peculiar to the coconut shy. It is white on red and consists entirely of

appliqué work. The exuberant character of the lettering, like that above the rifle range, and the robust flourishes on the dart booth, are in the Baroque tradition.

The decoration of the fairground show booth combines carved scrolls, arabesques and swags which date from the introduction of the mechanical organ in 1895 with naive painted images which carry on a tradition already established when Hogarth made his engraving of Southwark Fair and depicted booths hung with painted cloths advertising the shows.

The small altar-like Gavioli organ (below, left) with its curved opening, hybrid columns, vigorous termes and turbulent angels, clearly shows the link between fairground ornament and Baroque church decoration. The modest organ on the right exhibits a combination of this influence and that of the related style of Art Nouveau. The flamboyant painted motif on the swinging boats is also unmistakably Baroque and unlike the contemporary adornment of canal barges.

southern Germany with their writhing excess of ornament, their asymmetrical flourishes, arabesques and C-shapes, their undulating broken pediments, their bizarre forms of urn and obelisk, their gesticulating statues, their blaze of gold and glass? Dopp's fronts take the form of the façades and altars of the Bavarian Baroque churches. They are divided into three or more bays, generally of two stages, surmounted by a parapet and pediment. The organ occupies the centre of the upper or lower stage and the whole is encrusted with carved ornament and adorned with statues which are obviously related to the nymphs of the Amalienburg and the pastoral figures of the Würzburg Residenz and of Pommersfelden.

The invention of the paper organ coincided with the appearance of the cinematograph, and organs were soon in demand to accompany the 'Bioscope' shows which at the turn of the century became the most popular of fairground entertainments. But by about 1907 or 1908 permanent 'Living Picture' halls were springing up in every town, and to compete with these the fairground showmen enhanced the opulence and glamour of their fronts and loaded their merry-go-rounds with ever more extravagant embellishments. The organ was the centre and cynosure of all this ostentation. A typical Gavioli organ of this period exhibits a front of vigorous projections and recessions divided into five bays by giant columns carved with scaly, long-tailed beasts, and crowned with a parapet and semicircular pediment upon which four life-size, trumpet-blowing angels with violently agitated robes appear to have just alighted. Niches, roundels, and incredibly exaggerated acanthus sprays and grotesques fill the spaces between the columns. The organ pipes corrugate a scrolled opening in the lower stage and six dancing maidens lean forward in front of them holding up heavy garlands of fruit and flowers. They pirouette on bases decorated with snarling lion masks, adding the counterpoint of their revolutions to the upward sweep and the advancing and retreating movement of the whole design.

While figures like these, in flowing classical draperies, and statues of musicians and dancers in pastoral early eighteenth-century costume appear on many Edwardian organ fronts, they are often replaced by images of plump girls wearing contemporary dress or undress. The florid ornament preserves its Baroque flavour, mingling it now and then with an Art Nouveau motif—a female head swaying among drooping leaves on the end of a sinuous stem or a heart framed by waving tulips.

The total visual effect of the fairground at its zenith is of an art as frenzied and as prodigiously energetic as the most barbaric display of Baroque in southern Italy, Spain or Mexico. The merry-go-round in particular makes an impact which can only be compared to that of the amazing stucco work in the Cathedral at Agrigento, the façades of the Sagarario Metropolitano in Mexico City or the riotous frontispiece of Santi Nicola and Cataldo at Lecce. The original company of fiery, gaudily caparisoned gallopers has been swollen by a host of fantastic beasts and birds, griffins, chimeras, centaurs, dragons, rocs and mermaids, strange as the denizens of Bomarzo. But more bizarre, more riveting than any of these, is the heart of the structure, the organ and its figures, with, above it, a column of Cyclopean proportions, the soaring revolving centre encased in carved and gilded panels, studded with swags, masks and scrolls and surmounted by an immense crown-like capital, entirely covered with robust decoration, fringed with preposterous pendants, impelled into yet more delirious motion by shrill touches of metallic lustre and mirror glass, tossing back the images of barley-sugar brass (the characteristic Baroque pillar split into a hundred parts), and of the riders on their nightmarish steeds, gyrating, rising and falling.

Here, where art combines with the machine, the rhythm and movement sought by the great artists of the Baroque reaches an hysterical climax. Here, on the fairground is the true, belated revival of the only style which, except for the faintest, rarest echoes, was never emulated by the serious English and American architect in an age consisting almost wholly of revivals.

YOU are defired to Accompany the Corps of Mrs. *Elizabeth Cordiner*, from her late Dweling Houfe on *Afton's Quay*, to St. *Andrew's* Church, on *Wednefday* the 4th. of this Inftant *May*, 1746, percifely at Five o Clock in the Afternoon.

Popular Printing

BY JOHN LEWIS

POPULAR PRINTING can be defined as printing to be read by the man in the street. It began with proclamations, notices and almanacks. Richard Pynson in 1497 issued from his press in the City of London *The Shepheards Kalender*, but it was not until two hundred years later that Francis Moore's *Vox Stellarum* appeared. This was the forerunner of *Old Moore's Almanack*. This early popular printing is historically interesting, but visually rather dull. In the eighteenth century engravers such as Hogarth, Gravelot and Darly were busily employed in producing trade cards, letter-heads and invitation cards to weddings and funerals. For the latter, the full panoply of winged Time, with scythe and hour-glass and the Three Fates, Clotho, Lachesis and Atropos, would send some well-endowed corpse on its way. The less-well-off had to make do with a funerary woodcut such as that shown at the head of this page.

Poor Richard, 1736.

A N

Almanack

For the Year of Chrift

1 7 3 6,

Being *BISSEXTILE* or LEAP YEAR

And makes fince the Creation	Years
By the Account of the Eaftern *Greeks*	7244
By the Latin Church, when ☉ ent. ♈	6935
By the Computation of *W. W.*	5745
By the *Roman* Chronology	5685
By the *Jewifh* Rabbies	5497

Wherein is contained,

The Lunations, Eclipfes, Judgment of the Weather, Spring Tides, Planets Motions & mutual Afpects, Sun and Moon's Rifing and Setting, Length of Days, Time of High Water, Fairs, Courts, and obfervable Days.

Fitted to the Latitude of Forty Degrees, and a Meridian of Five Hours Weft from *London*, but may without fenfible Error, ferve all the adjacent Places, even from *Newfoundland* to *South-Carolina*.

By *RICHARD SAUNDERS*, Philom.

PHILADELPHIA:

Printed and fold by *B. FRANKLIN*, at the New Printing-Office near the Market.

1736. *Poor Richard's Almanack* printed and published by Benjamin Franklin

THE WHOLE
LIFE and TRIAL
AT LARGE
Of the Notorious Highwayman
Richard Turpin,

At *York* Affizes, on the 22d Day of *March*, 1739, before the Hon. Sir WILLIAM CHAPPLE, Knt. Judge of Affize, and one of His Majefty's Juftices of the Court of *King's Bench.*

Taken down in Court by Mr. THOMAS KYLL, Profeffor of Short-Hand.

To which is prefix'd,

An exact Account of the faid *Turpin*, from his firft coming into *Yorkshire*, to the Time of his being committed Prifoner to *York* Caftle ; communicated by Mr. APPLETON of *Beverly*, Clerk of the Peace for the *Eaft-Riding* of the faid County.

With a Copy of a Letter which *Turpin* received from his Father, while under Sentence of Death.

To which is added,

His Behaviour at the Place of Execution, on *Saturday* the 7th of *April*, 1739. Together with the whole Confeffion he made to the Hangman at the Gallows; wherein he acknowledg'd himfelf guilty of the Facts for which he fuffer'd, own'd the Murder of Mr. *Thompfon's* Servant on *Epping-Foreft*, and gave a particular Account of feveral Robberies which he had committed.

POOR RICHARD'S ALMANACK, which first appeared in Philadelphia in 1732 was only the second Almanack to be printed in the United States of America. Its publisher-author was Benjamin Franklin who used the pseudonym of Richard Saunders. Benjamin Franklin was also the printer of the Almanack which continued in production until 1757.

The account of Dick Turpin's trial, the front page of which appears above, is a very modest forerunner of the horrific street literature of Jemmy Catnach, who was working in Seven Dials in London about eighty years after the execution of Turpin.

John Lightbody sculp.

Mr. John Alderſon.

Printed on the River of THAMES when Frozen over,

JANUARY 21, 1739 40.

1739/40. Engraved and letterpress printed on the frozen river Thames

A true and exact LIST of all the HORSES, &c.

That are ENTER'D to RUN

On Kersall Moor, near Manchester,

On *Wednesday* the 21st, *Thursday* the 22d, and *Friday* the 23d of *October* 1761.

On *Wednesday* the 21st, for 50l. by four Year olds carrying 8 ft. five Year olds 8 st. 8 lb. six Year olds 9 ft. 5 lb. and aged Horses 10 st. Saddle and Bridle included, four Mile Heats.

Philip Egerton, Esqrs. Bay Mare, *Rockatina*, 5 Years old, Rider Robert Collins, in Blue.
Mr. Pearson's Chesnut Mare, *Lashing Molly*, 5 Years old, Rider John Cotesworth, in Green.
William Broome, Esqrs. Bay Horse, *Hector*, 6 Years old, Rider unknown.

On *Thursday* the 22d, for a Whim Plate of 50l. by Horses, &c. 14 Hands to carry 9 ft. higher or lower Weight in Proportion, and all under 7 Years old to be allowed 7 lb. Weight for each Year, according to their Ages, four Mile Heats.

Mr. Williams's Bay Horse, *Moscow*, 6 Years olds, 14 Hands 1 Inch 3-qrs. 9 ft. 5 lb. 4 Oz. Rider Robert Collins, in Blue.
Mr. Stanhope's Bay Horse, *Short Hose*, Aged, 14 Hands, 9 ft. Rider Thomas Clough, in Blue.
Dr. Bracken's Chesnut Horse, *Dismal*, 6 Years old, 14 Hands, 8 st. 8 lb. 12 Oz. Rider Matt. Wilson, in Red.
Mr. Eyre's Chesnut Mare, *Pretty Bess*, 5 Years old, 14 Hands 3 Inches, 7 ft. 7 lb. Rider John Eyre, in Red, (To be Sold)

And on *Friday* the 23d, for 50l. by six Year olds carrying 9 ft. 7 lb. and Aged Horses 10 st. Saddle and Bridle included, four Mile Heats.

Philip Egerton, Esqrs. Bay Horse, *Dismfast*. Aged, Rider Robert Collins, in Blue.
Mr. Peter's Bay Horse, *Orphen*, 6 Years old, Rider Robert Bloss, in Yellow.
William Broome, Esqrs. Bay Horse, *Hector*, 6 Years old, Rider unknown.
Mr. Williams's Bay Horse, *Moscow*, 6 Years old, Rider unknown.

To start at Twelve o'Clock. There will be an Ordinary every Day immediately after the Races, provided by Mr. Bodworth, in the Exchange which will be properly air'd for the Purpose.

The HORSE RACE, a Poem

THE Signal giv'n by a shrill Trumpet's Sound,
The Coursers start, and scour along the Ground:
While for the Palm the straining Steeds contend,
Beneath their Hoofs the Grass doth scarcely bend;
So long and smooth their strokes, so swift they pass,
That the Spectators of the noble Race
Can scarce distinguish by their doubtful Eye,
If on the Ground they run, or in the Air they fly.
O'er Hills and Dales the speedy Coursers fly,
And with thick Clouds of Dust obscure the Sky,

With clashing Whips the furious Riders tear
Their Coursers Sides, and wound th'afflicted Air,
On their thick Manes the stooping Riders lie,
Press forward, and would fain their Steeds outfly.
By Turns they are behind, by Turns before;
Their Flanks and Sides all bath'd in Sweat and Gore,
Such Speed the Steeds, such Zeal the Riders shew,
To reach bright Fame that swift before them flew,
Upon the last, with spurning Heels the first
Cast Storms of Sand, and smoth'ring Clouds of Dust;
The hindmost strain their Nerves, and snort and blow,
And their white Foam upon the foremost throw.

MANCHESTER: Printed by Jos. HARROP, opposite the Exchange, by Order of the STEWARDS.

1761. Race Bill printed in Manchester

IN THE very hard winter of 1739–40 the Thames was frozen over above London Bridge. All kinds of stalls did a lively trade in selling hot chestnuts, baked potatoes, mulled wines and neguses, and at least one enterprising printer set up his press on the ice. The engraving opposite would have been printed beforehand. The race bill for the Kersall Moor Meeting was printed in 1761 and set a style that was followed for the next century.

The LIFE, *and* SUFFERINGS *of*

Jane Wade, a young Lady of Pleasure and Fashion,

Who was Seduced from Home, at the age of Sixteen, by a rich Gentleman, who kept her in London. Also an account of her un-happy Death in a House of Ill Fame, with a Copy of a Letter she Wrote to her Parents on her Death Bed, which she requested might be forwarded to them immediately after she expired

A Copy of Affecting

VERSES.

ALL maidens young awhile attend
  And listen unto me,
While I rehearse in humble verse
  My woes and misery.
And if you take the good advice
  Which now to you is told,
Account the gift of greater price
  Than if I gave you gold.

A miller's daughter I was born,
  An honest man was he,
Who labour'd hard, for to maintain,
  A numerous family.
But when I reach'd my sixteenth year
  As you the truth shall know,
A doctor young, with flattering tongue
  Did prove my overthrow.

Unto my father's house he came,
  (Curse on his perjur'd arts)
And there with sighs, and vows, and lies,
  He gain'd my virgin heart.
His wily tongue did me persuade,
  From my father's house to flee,
And many a solemn oath he made
  That he would marry me.

At ball and plays, and operas
  I cut a dashing show,
In satins drest and all the rest,
  So smart from top to toe.
For he had plenty at command
  And was an only son;

Whate'er I wish'd if I express'd
  That instant it was done.
In vain I urg'd him to perform
  What he so oft had swore,
Till he told me plain, if I ask'd again
  He'd see my face no more.
Before a twelvemonth had elaps'd,
  He met a fairer face,
And me forsook, quite destitute,
  In sorrow and disgrace.

Compell'd to go upon the town,
  How bitter was my fate,
And now disease has pull'd me down
  And death is at the gate.
Behold me now, ye pretty maids,
  And see what I endure
And learn to shun false-flattering tongues
  Lest my hard fate be yours.

She then for Pen and Paper call'd
  Upon her dying bed,
And to her tender parents wrote
  Most pitiful indeed,
O such a Letter she did write
  As griev'd their hearts full sore,
But when the same they had perus'd
  Their daughter was no more.

Low in the silent dust she sleeps
  Her earthly sufferings o'er,
And left her parents dear to weep
  And her sad fate deplore.
The wretch who worked her downfall
  May prosper for a time,
But vengeance like a lion yet
  Shall overtake his crime.

JANE WADE was the eldest daughter of James Wade, a respectable Miller near Rye. About 2 years ago, [...] in her sixteenth year, she by chance attracted the attention of [...] rich and profligate young Doctor, who was residing for the recovery of his health, near Mr. Wade's mill. He introduced himself to her, and by dint of handsome presents, and a thousand fine stories of wedlock, &c. he persuaded her to elope with him and come to London. As he had an ample fortune, and was no economist he kept her in the first style of fashion, visited all places of amusement, with servants to wait upon her, and the most costly clothes, and trinkets. After leading this sort of life for about a twelvemonth, he got tired of her, and it was not long before he abandoned her altogether, and went to France with another girl whom chance threw in his way. Jane was now destitute, without money or friends, and ashamed to return to her Parents, she was driven upon the town, when after enduring all the miseries of protistation for twelvemonths, she died a miserable death in a common brothel.

abandoned me; and not having the means of returning home I was forced for a subsistence to wander the streets as a common prostitute, which dreadful course of life, brought on incurable disorders which alas! proved fatal and has brought me to an early grave. It is my last request that you will acquaint my dear mother cautiously of my death, and tell her not to regret the loss of one who had she lived would only have disgraced her old age.—Oh! my dear parents it grieves me to my very heart, to think of my misconduct, but pray for me & may the GOD of HEAVEN protect and bless you; and pray advise my late Companions to take a warning by my miserable fate, and to return to the paths of righteousness.

Stretched upon a death-bed, I now look back upon my mispent life, and Oh! how bitter is the reflection. I trust that my sad downfall, and miserable death will be a warning to all young thoughtless girls, not to suffer them selves to be deceived and decoyed from the paths of virtue With dying hand, I subscribe myself dear and honoured parents.   Your miserable child.
                                                                    Jane Wade.

THE FOLLOWING IS A

Copy of a Letter

She wrote while on her Death Bed, to her Parents and Friends.

My Dear Parents,

Before this meet your eyes, your unfortunate Jane will be no more. I am sorry to name what was the cause of my early and miserable dissolution but it is necessary that I discover to you that I was ensnared and led astray by a deceitful young man who effected my ruin and

THE hour of my departure's come,
  I hear the voice that calls me home
Now, O my God, let trouble cease
And let the sinner die in peace.

Not in my innocence I trust
I bow before thee in the dust.
But through my Saviour's blood alone,
I look for mercy at thy throne.

My hope is fix'd on him on high,
  To Him I look, to Him I cry,
Stretch forth Thine everlasting arms,
And shield me in the last alarms.

The hour of my departure's come,
  I hear the voice that calls me home
Now, O my God, let trouble cease
And let the sinner die in peace.

J. Catnach, Printer, 2, Monmouth-court, 7 Dials

c. 1825. Street literature, printed by J. Catnach

c. 1840. Stock block

I T WAS NOT until the beginning of the nineteenth century
when a wide range of display letters came into use that
popular printing really came to life. There was not only this
wealth of letter forms, but also woodcut illustrations which
could be produced cheaply and printed at the same time as the
typematter. Many of these vivid little cuts were sold by the typefounders as stock material.

In 1816 Jemmy Catnach, perhaps the greatest of 'popular
printers', set up as a printer of street literature in the Seven Dials
near St Giles' Church in London. This street literature mainly
consisted of either song sheets or the 'Last Dying Confessions'
of convicted felons or gruesome descriptions of murders. In
1819 Catnach was sentenced to six months in the Clerkenwell
House of Correction for suggesting a pie maker called Pizzey
made his pies from human bodies. In 1824 the famous murder
by William Corder of Maria Marten, whose remains he buried
in a red barn in Polstead in Suffolk, resulted in a handsome
piece of business for Catnach. He sold 1,166,000 copies of the
murderer's 'Last Dying Speech'. Catnach used various engravers,
including the great Northumbrian engraver Thomas Bewick,
both for his street literature and for his farthing, halfpenny and
penny children's books.

c. 1840 Typefounders' stock blocks ranged in size from these spirited engravings down to cuts of little ships, railway engines, etc., that measured less than half an inch across.

Discovery of an Extraordinary
MURDER
Committed by a Respectable Miller, of Wittam in Berkshire,

Upon the body of his sweetheart, in December last, he first by false promises seduced her, and got her with child, after which under the pretence of taking a walk and settling when they should be married. He led her into a field, and struck her with a stick and beat her till she lay a corpse before him; He then threw her into the River. The young woman being missed he was suspected; but as no proof could be brought, he was allowed to go upon bail. But the very day before the assizes, her body was found floating before her Father's door, at Hensey Ferry, when he was again brought up, sent for Trial; and the facts so fully proved that he was found guilty, and condemned to die; since which he has made a full confession of the fact.

YOUNG men & maidens give ear
  Unto what I shall now relate,
O mark you well & you shall hear,
  Of my unhappy fate.
Near famous Oxford town,
  I first did draw my breath
O that I had been cast away,
  In an untimely birth.

My tender parents brought me up,
  Provided for me well,
And in the town of Wittam then,
  They placed me in a mill.
By chance upon an Oxford lass,
  I cast a wanton eye,
And promis'd I would marry her
  If she with me would lie.

But to the world I do declare,
  With sorrow grief and woe,
This folly brought us in a snare,
  And wrought our overthrow.
For the damsel came to me & said,
  By you I am with child,
I hope dear John you'll mary me
  For you have me defiled.

Soon after that her mother came,
  As you shall understand,
And often times did me persuade,
  To wed her out of hand.
And thus perplex'd on every side,
  I could no comfort find,
So to make away with this creature,
  A thought came in my mind.

About a month since Christmas, last,
  Oh, cursed be the day,
e devil then did me persuade,
  To take her life away.

I called her from her sister's door,
  At eight o'clock at night,
Poor creature she did little dream,
  I owed her any spite.

I told her if she'd walk with me,
  Aside a little way
We both together would agree,
  About our wedding day.
Thus I deluded her again,
  Into a private place,
Then took a stick out of the hedge
  And struck her in the face.

But she fell on her bended knee,
  And did for mercy cry,
For heaven's sake don't murder me;
  I am not fit to die.
But I on her no pity took,
  But wounded her full sore,
Until her life away I took,
  Which I can ne'er restore.

With many grievous shrieks & cries
  She did resign her breath,
Thus in an inhuman barbarous sort,
  I put my love to death.
And then I took her by the hair
  To cover the foul sin,
And dragged her to the river side,
  Then threw her body in.

Thus in the blood of innocence,
  My hands were deeply dy'd,
And stained in her purple gore,
  That should have been my bride.
Then home unto my mill I ran,
  But sorely was amazed,   (done
My man he thought I had mischief
  And strangely on me gaz'd.

Oh, what's the matter then said he,
  You look as pale as death,   (so
What makes you shake and tremble
  As though you'd lost your breath.
How came you by that blood upon,
  Your trembling hands and clothes,

Presently to him I replied
  By bleeding at the nose.

I wishfully upon him look'd
  But little to him said,
I snatch'd the candle from his hand,
  And went unto my bed.
There I lay trembling all the night,
  For I could take no rest,
And perfect flames of hell did flash,
  Like lightning in my face.

Next day the damsel being miss'd,
  And no where to be found,
Then I was apprehended soon,
  And to the assizes bound.
Her sister did again me swear,
  She reason had no doubt,
That I had made away with her,
  Because I called her out.

But Satan did me still persuade
  I stiffly did deny,
Quoth he there's no witness can,
  Against thee testify.
Now when her mother did her cry,
  I scoffingly did say,
On purpose then to frighten me,
  She sent her child away.

I publish'd in the post then,
  My wickedness to blind,
Five guineas any one should have,
  That could her body find.
But heaven had a watchful eye,
  And brought it so about,
That tho' I stiffly did deny,
  This murder will come out.

The very day before the assizes,
  Her body it was found,
Floating before her father's door,
  At Hindley Ferry Town.
So I a second time was seiz'd,
  To Oxford bound with speed,
And here examined again,
  About the bloody deed.

Now the Coroner and Jury both,
  Together did agree,
That this damsel was made away,
  And murdered by me.
The justice too perceived the guilt,
  Nor either would take bail,
But the next morning I was sent,
  Away to Reading goal.

When I was brought before the judge
  My man did testify,
That blood upon my hand & clothes,
  That night he did espy.
The judge he told the jury then,
  The circumstance was plain,

Look on the prisoner at the bar,
  He has this creature slain.

About the murder at the first,
  The jury did divide,
But when they brought their verdict
  All of them guilty cry'd.   (in
The jailor took and bound me strait,
  As soon as I was cast,
And then within the prison strong
  He there did lay me fast.

With fetters strong then I was bound
  And shin too bolted was I,
Yet I the murder would not own,
  But did it still deny.
My father did on me prevail,
  My kindred all likewise
To own the murder which I did
  To them with watery eyes.

My father then he said to me
  Saying, my son, oh, why,
Have you brought yourself to shame,
  And all your family.
Father I own the crimes I did,
  I guilty am indeed
Which cruel fact I must confess.
  Doth make my heart to bleed.

The worst of death I do deserve,
  My crime it is so base,
For I no mercy shewed to her,
  Most wretched is my case.
Lord grant me grace while I do stay
  That I may now repent,
Before I from this wicked world,
  Most shamefully am sent.

Young men take warning now by me
  All filthy lusts defy
By giving way to wickedness,
  Alas! this day I die.
Lord wash my hateful sins away,
  Which have been manifold,
Have mercy on me Lord I pray,
  And Christ receive my soul.

J. Catnach, Printer, 2 & 3, Monmouth-court, 7 Dials

c. 1830. Street literature printed by J. Catnach

THEATRE ROYAL.

BY HIS MAJESTY'S SERVANTS.

MISS MACAULEY'S

Third Night.

On THURSDAY, Feb. 15, 1821,

WILL BE PERFORMED THE TRAGEDY, OF

Jane Shore.

Gloster, Mr. SMITH.
Lord Hastings, Mr. VINING.—Belmour, Mr. DIDDEAR.
Ratcliffe, Mr. BEACHAM.
Dumont, Mr. T. SHORT.—Catesby, Mr. G. SMITH.
Derby, Mr. CLIFFORD.

Jane Shore, Miss MACAULEY.
Alicia, Mrs. W. CLIFFORD.

IN THE COURSE OF THE EVENING,
The celebrated Musical Recitation of

LORD ULLIN's DAUGHTER

BY MISS MACAULEY.

AFTER WHICH THE MELO-DRAMA OF

RUGANTINO;

Or, the Bravo of Venice.

Andreas, (Duke of Venice) Mr. SMITH
Lomellino; Mr. CLIFFORD—Manfrone, Mr. WILLIAMS
Parozzi, Mr. BEACHAM
Memmo, Mr. BENNETT.—Rugantino,, Mr. T. SHORT.
Contarino, Mr. DIDDEAR
Stephano, Mr. HAMERTON.—Falieri, Mr. G. SMITH.
Bertoldo, Mr. G. NICHOLLS.
Juanillo, Mr. STACEY.—Pisani, Mr. C. NICHOLLS.

Rosabella, Miss MACAULEY.

Camilla, Mrs. JONES.—Laura, Mrs. HAMERTON.

1821. Playbill with eight different display typefaces

U U stands for Umbrella, that
upset Sammy Snub. u

c. 1832. Illustration to one of Catnach's children's books

TYPOGRAPHICALLY the circus bills and play bills made the best use of the new type forms. Typefounders on either side of the Atlantic vied with each other in the variety and fantasy of these display letters. It must have been a pretty heady experience for the popular printer to have at his disposal this wealth of typographic material. Bills and posters, labels, letterheads and tickets suddenly took on a new life. The play bills (opposite and overleaf) show the development during the first half of the century in the use of these typefaces. The Theatre Royal bill of 1821 makes a modest use of a bold fat face, a shaded and a decorated letter, but the American bill overleaf has moved a long way in the weight and variety of its letters. By the mid-century, a vivid vernacular had become established, not only for play bills, but also for auctioneer's notices and for anything else to do with trade. This vernacular was an expression of unsophisticated tradesmen who achieved something approaching an art form with their posters and bills.

Broadsheets of parlour games were another manifestation of the art. The illustration on page 99 is from one of a series of sheets called 'Nuts to Crack', printed and published by R. MacDonald in London in about the middle of the nineteenth century. A rebus nearly always filled the centre of these sheets; the rest was taken up with Conundrums, Enigmas, Charades, Puzzles and Riddles.

1854. Playbill printed in Philadelphia, showing no less than twenty different varieties and sizes of display letter

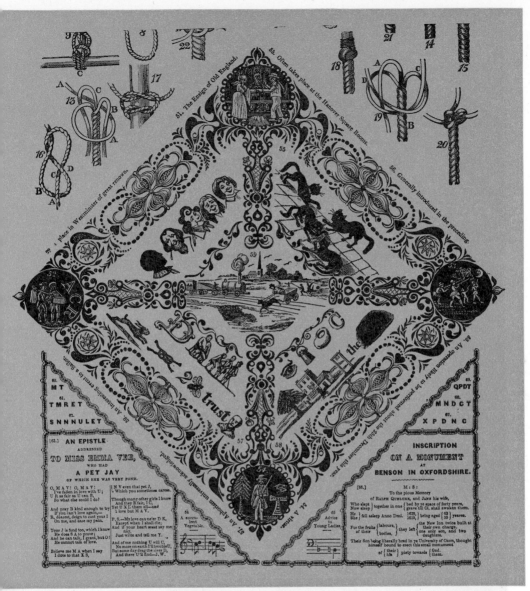

1845. Part of a 'Nuts to Crack' broadsheet

Much of this popular printing is a reflection of the manners and moods of the time. Overleaf are two bills, one for J. W. Beecher an exuberant Spitalfields draper, crying his wares as if he was a stallholder in a market, the other for W. Endall, an auctioneer from Henley-in-Arden, announcing that he has been engaged to sell the wherewithal of a couple of bankrupts! Mr Endall's punchy typography is a match for Beecher's Cockney humour.

ONCE TRY—YOU'LL COME AGAIN!
TO
J. W. BEECHER'S
SLAP UP TOG
AND OUT AND OUT
KICKSIES BUILDER,
No. 186, Brick Lane,
Spitalfields, Next Door to the "Laurel Tree,"
And Sign of the "Golden Fleece."

Mr B. nabs the chance of putting his customers awake that he has just made his escape from Italy, not forgetting to clap his mawleys upon some of the right sort of stuff, when on his return home he was stunned to find one of the top Manufacturers of Manchester had cut his lucky, and stepped off to the Swan Stream, leaving behind him a valuable stock of Moleskius Cords, Velveteens, Box Cloths, Plushes, Doe Skins, Pilots, &c., and having some ready in his kick grabbed the chance—stepped home with the swag—and is now safely landed at his crib. He can turn out Toggery very slap at the following low prices for

Ready Gilt—Tick being No go.

Upper Benjamins, built on a downy plan, a monarch to half a finnuff. Fishing or Shooting Togs, cut slap, 1 pound, 1 quarter and a peg. A Fancy Sleeve Blue Plush or Pilot ditto, made very saucy, a couter. Pair of Kerseymere or Doeskin Kicksies, built very slap with the artful dodge, a canary. Pair of Bath or Worsted Cords, cut to drop down on the trotters, a quid. Pair of out and out Cords, built very serious, 9 bob and a kick. Pair of stout Broad built in the Melton Mowbray style, half a sov. Pair of Moleskins, built hanky spanky, with a double fakement down the sides and artful buttons at bottom, half a monarch.

Mud Pipes, Knee Caps and Trotter Cases built very low.

A decent allowance made to Seedy Swells, Tea Kettle Purgers, Head Robbers, and Flunkeys out of Collar.
N.B.—Gentlemen finding their own Broady can be accommodated.

MAKE NO MISTAKE!
No. 186, Brick Lane,
SPITALFIELDS.

Stutter, Printer, 76, Church Street, Bethnal Green.

c. 1860. Draper and Outfitter's notice

FREEHOLDS

AT

GREAT ALNE.

VOTES for South WARWICKSHIRE.

In re Rufford and Wragge's Bankruptcy.

To be Sold by Auction,

BY W. ENDALL

AT THE ANGEL INN, ALCESTER,

On TUESDAY, the 29th day of NOVEMBER, 1853,

At 2 o'Clock in the Afternoon, under Conditions to be then produced;

ALL THOSE TWO FREEHOLD

COTTAGES

Or TENEMENTS, containing each, 2 Chambers, Kitchen and Pantry, joint Brewhouse, and Pump of capital Water, 2 Pigstyes, and

GARDENS;

Situate by the side of the road leading from Spernal to Little Alne, at Burford's Lane, in the Parish of Great Alne, in the County of Warwick; adjoining the Estates of Sir ROBERT THROCKMORTON, and the Trustees of M. MILLS, Esq., and now in the respective occupations of William Court and George Hawkes.

For particulars apply to Mr. William MURRAY, Solicitor, London Street, Fenchurch Street, London; Mr. HARWARD, Solicitor, Stourbridge; Mr. WHITMORE, Official Assignee, Birmingham; or the Auctioneer, Henley-in-Arden.

PRINTED AT THE OFFICES OF THE AUCTIONEER HENLEY-IN-ARDEN

1853. Auctioneer's bill

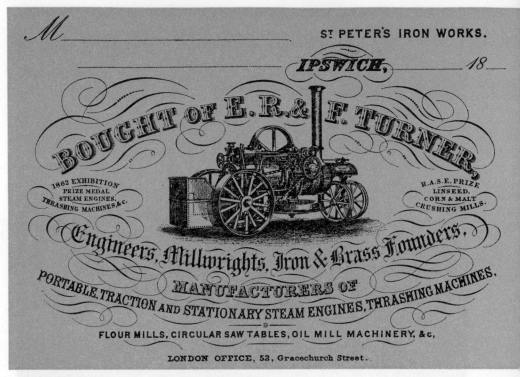

Mᵉ_____ St PETER'S IRON WORKS.

IPSWICH, 18___

BOUGHT OF E. R. & F. TURNER,

1862 EXHIBITION
PRIZE MEDAL
STEAM ENGINES,
THRASHING MACHINES &c.

R.A.S.E. PRIZE
LINSEED,
CORN & MALT
CRUSHING MILLS.

Engineers, Millwrights, Iron & Brass Founders,

MANUFACTURERS OF

PORTABLE, TRACTION AND STATIONARY STEAM ENGINES, THRASHING MACHINES,

FLOUR MILLS, CIRCULAR SAW TABLES, OIL MILL MACHINERY, &c,

LONDON OFFICE, 52, Gracechurch Street.

c. 1880. Engraved billhead printed by lithography

POPULAR PRINTING has its moments of refinement. The engravers of the eighteenth-century trade cards took advantage of all the extravagances of the Rococo, Chinoiserie and Gothick movements. By the mid-nineteenth century the lithographer and the wood-engraver and the letterpress printer had ousted the copper-engraver from the world of billheads and trade cards. The engraved style still persisted, either drawn on the stone or transferred from the copper plate. The 'Portable Traction Engine Manufacturer's' letter-head above was engraved in the 1860's and then transferred to the lithographic stone. The New Jersey Paper Mill label, on the other hand, is a straightforward and very competent bit of wood-engraving. The engraver was Alexander Anderson, who was a close follower of Bewick. In fact in 1802 Anderson published from New York his plagiarised facsimile copy of Bewick's *Quadrupeds*. He followed this with various imitations of English work, but much of his time was spent on cutting blocks for labels for soap, tooth powder, ink and other commodities. Anderson was a brilliant craftsman and particularly strong on the American Eagle, of which he engraved innumerable variations.

102

1850. Papermill label engraved by Alexander Anderson

Nᴜᴍᴇʀᴏᴜs anonymous craftsmen on both sides of the Atlantic engraved blocks for every kind of popular printing. I have seen a version of the wood-burning locomotive above (a stock block from the Mackellar Smith's and Jordan Typefoundry of Philadelphia) advertising Real Estate at Palo Alto in California and the Chinoiserie block from Caslon and Livermore used on a Suffolk grocer's tea bag. These prints from stock blocks are just one aspect of Popular Printing, an infinitely fascinating subject for study or collection.

Street Games in Southwark

BY FRED BASON

DO YOU KNOW that wonderful book, *London Street Games* by Norman Douglas? I have been looking at it to refresh my memory of the games I used to play with my pals in the streets of Southwark, where I was born in the year 1907 (and where I still live—at number 4 Broadmayne, in Portland Street, S.E.17).

I was an unwanted child, being born when my mother was forty-one. I had no brothers or sisters. So I spent most of my time, when I'd finished my home-work (which included cleaning knives, forks and spoons and my mother's shoes) playing in the streets with my friends. They didn't like my mother, because she was always confiscating the balls that fell into our basement and she wouldn't give them back to the kids until they apologised—and no child in Southwark liked to apologise.

Anyway, my friends would stand outside and shout: 'Mother's got a nasty cough; Father's got the gout. Old Freddie Bason, are you coming out?' They shouted so loud that at last my mother would tell me to stop my home-work and join them. Then we began to play our traditional games.

'Queenie' or 'Kingie' was a most popular ball game because any number could play it. It was called 'Queenie' when girls played it, and 'Kingie' when there were more boys than girls in the game. This game's charm lay in the fact that not only could any number of children play in one game but it did not need either skill or luck, and it didn't even need a real ball. Newspaper folded up and tied with string would do—or a ping-pong ball or a small piece of wood just big enough to hide in one's hand or up one's jersey or down one's knickers. 'Queenie' stood on the pavement with her back to the street. In the street were her subjects. She would throw the ball over her head into the street where someone would have to catch it. As soon as it was caught 'Queenie' would call out 'one, two, three, Queenie' and turn round. All her subjects had their hands behind their backs. 'Queenie' had to guess which one had the ball. She had three guesses, and if she guessed right she still remained 'Queenie'. If she failed, the boy or girl having the ball became 'Queenie'. It was a good game because it could last for hours.

'Teaser' was a ball game only three could play. On either side of the street stood a boy. In the centre was another boy. The boy on one side had to throw the ball over the head of the boy in the middle to the boy on the other side of the street. But if the boy in the centre was able to get it before it reached the other boy then he won and the boy who had failed to get the ball became 'Teaser'. And you *could* be teased, because some rough boys threw it *at you* instead of over your head—and you had to dodge out of the way quickly and had no chance of catching it.

There was another ball game called 'Hot Rice'. Up to eight children played this game, which could be very rough. The leader of the gang would say, pointing at each person in turn, and including himself, 'Eanie—Meanie—Miny—Mo'. 'Mo' dropped out. Eventually there would be only two left. Still 'Eanie, Meanie, Miny, Mo'—between two children left; one when it came to 'Mo'. 'Mo' had the ball and the last one was 'Hot Rice'. The rest of the children had to hit him with the ball. There was a limited space within which you could run—usually between two lampposts. You had to be very nimble to avoid being hit. The drawback to this game was that no one was ever keen to be 'Hot Rice', and once 'Hot Rice' was hit the game seemed to be over. After all, though it might be fun to hit another boy (or girl) with a ball, if the penalty for hitting him made you 'Hot Rice' then unless you were extremely nimble or very brave you were inclined to miss him. Of course, it had to be a near miss or you would be judged a coward or a bad sport or a stinking thrower!

'Dead-man's Cap' was another rough game. It was only played by boys, and they had to have caps. It was played rather in the same way as 'Queenie', but the boys stood in a line some three feet apart, behind each other. The 'Dead-man' threw his cap over his shoulder. One of the other boys had to catch it—

and hide it quickly. The 'Dead-man' had to guess or discover who had the cap. If he guessed right he had to return to the spot where he started from before the boy with the cap hit him with it. And a peaked cap could really hurt—especially if the other boys obstructed your run 'home'.

Girls had a lovely game called 'Alley Gobs'. I do not ever recall seeing any boys play it. 'Alley Gobs'? Well, the 'gobs' were four small square stones about one inch across. The 'alley' was usually a coloured glass marble. The gobs were placed on the ground close to the player. She threw the alley up and recaught it as she picked up one gob. Then she threw the alley up and picked up two gobs. In the final action all four gobs were picked up as the alley was caught. A real champion could do it all with one hand! I do not know if gobs are made now-a-days but I have in 1970 seen girls still playing 'Alley Gobs'; maybe they were a relic of their mother's schooldays.

There was a variation of 'Alley Gobs' and it was usually called 'Five Stones' or 'Bouncer'. The stones were just ordinary small sea-shore pebbles and the bouncer a small rubber ball, about the same size as a golf ball (often an actual old golf ball was used) which had an extremely good bounce. The ball was bounced and a stone was picked up. It was returned to the ground and two stones were picked up at the second bounce. This was continued till all five stones were picked up. There was a variation in this game when the ball was allowed to bounce once as one stone was picked up and bounced five times before picking up five stones. To wait for a ball to bounce five times, then catch it and pick up five stones with the other hand, was no mean feat. The ball had to be thrown down with terrific force in order to get five bounces out of it before you caught it. Keeping an eye on the ball for one second and then glancing down to where the five stones lay in another second was a real art. Of course the winner was the one who made no mistakes in the series of moves. Girls used to play this game for hours—all innocent fun.

The sex education of children today has taken all the fun out of playing 'Doctors and Nurses'. When I was a little boy we had no sex education whatsoever. But I learnt several anatomy lessons from playing 'Doctors'. We could seldom get a patient; so the nurse was our patient. It was all good fun and usually ended up with the Doctor giving the nurse a tickle where she was most ticklish. I never heard of any child in my part of London coming to any harm whatsoever by playing 'Doctors and Nurses'. 'Mothers and Fathers' was almost the same game—because mother got ill and father had to examine her to find out what was wrong. (Nurse had caught some disease and the Doctor had to find out what was diseased.)

Most of the boys in Walworth owned a peg-top when I was ten years old. I asked six boys of Walworth recently and none had any idea what a peg-top was, so I assume they are no longer made. The best 'tops' were made from boxwood, and three-pence would pay for one that would last for years. Good string was wrapped around it, and at the flick of the wrist you pulled away the string and the top would spin on its steel-nail-like base. There were also peg-tops that one whipped round with a thin piece of leather on a stick. Humming tops were made of tin, having very elegant designs all over them. They made a pretty little tune as they hummed around. Sometimes they were made to spin with string, but mainly they had a small mechanical device at the top of the humming top which one pushed up and down until the whole twirled round. I always longed to own a a humming top, but they were priced from 2s. to 3s 6d. each, and were way beyond my parents' purse strings. However, my dad did buy me a hoop. It was made of iron, about four feet in diameter, and an inch wide. With a stick you knocked the hoop along—and you had to run to keep up with it. It never wore out. I grew tired of it and after two years' constant wear I swopped it for a penknife. This had a section for taking out stones from horses' hoofs, but I never found a horse needing my attention.

Vicious boys used to tie the tails of stray dogs together with string—or tin cans on to the tails of cats. But the police stamped out these games pretty quickly with on-the-spot justice, a thrashing—'and now tell your mother why I did it!' But they never told—and to be caught by a policeman let your side down. There was also a dangerous game called 'Bangers'.

You needed a large key, three or four live matches, a nail or piece of thick wire, and some string. Into the top of the key you rammed the live heads of three matches, then you jammed home a nail (the same size as the hole in the key) over the live heads and twisted the rest of the nail or wire round the key. Then a large piece of string was attached to the key at one end and the handle of the key at the other. The key would then be swung with great force against a wall and would explode with a startling noise. Boys were injured with pieces of it. If a teacher at school or the police found you with a large key you had to have a very good explanation, or you were in for a good hiding!

'Twisting' (or Twisters) was a game I never did like. Two children joined hands and twisted round and round. I always got dizzy. Mostly girls played this game, but when a boy and a girl played 'Twisters' they were usually fond of each other, and, having whirled round and round, they got dizzy and had a good reason to sit down, hold hands and do some kissing!

Until Park Keepers got wise there was a game called 'Steady Sticks'. One got all manner of sticks or branches off trees, usually about six inches long. They were placed on top of each other, and you had to remove some of them without any of the other sticks moving. It was not so easy as it seems; when the branches were odd shapes they seemed to cling together. But pulling off branches of the very few trees in Walworth was frowned upon not only by Park Keepers but by parents. (Tree climbing often split trousers!)

I've not seen them for many years outside a circus but both boys and girls made and played on stilts in my childhood days. Two planks of wood about four feet high, two blocks of wood nailed on, a foot from the base, and you walked along on the blocks. It was a good game—but making stilts was not at all easy. The wood usually came from long egg boxes, but it took ages to find blocks to nail on to them. A champion stilt-walker could hop along on one stilt for at least a hundred yards and was much admired. For some reason girls were not good on stilts.

'Gammy' or 'Broken Bottles' was a game of skill mostly played by girls. Four or five would stand in a ring and throw the ball to each other. If they failed to catch the ball they became 'Gammy'

('gammy' means awkward or lame) and forfeited the use of one hand—so they had to catch the ball with one hand. If they next failed to catch the ball they knelt on one knee—still trying to catch with one hand. Another failure to catch and they were down on both knees. If they failed to catch the ball in this almost impossible position they were 'out'. There was a variation whereby, having failed to catch the ball with two hands first time, you went on one knee but could still use both hands to catch the ball —then both knees on the floor but two hands in use—then with one hand behind your back you had to catch the ball or be 'out'. It really depended on the force with which a ball was thrown at you. If a ball was thrown at your face rather hard you were indeed Gammy, and didn't want to play any more! And little girls can be quite cruel at times. But I could never understand why it was called 'Broken Bottles'. On the other hand 'Knocking Down Ginger' did use a bottle and it was often broken. It was a good game, with a soft ball. 'Ginger' was either a tin or a bottle. (We used tough ginger-beer bottles.) The ball was aimed at 'Ginger', bounced against the wall, and you caught the ball after its bounce. It was an art to do *both*—knock down 'Ginger' and catch the ball on the rebound—and you *had* to be really 'Ginger' (which was the word for 'alert' when I was a lad) to play this game successfully.

I remember clearly the words of a ring game played fifty years ago:

> There was a King of York
> Who had ten thousand men
> He led them up to the top of a hill
> Then led them down again
> And when they were up they were up
> And when they were down they were down
> And when they were only half way up
> They were neither up nor down.

I remember the words—but for my life I don't remember how the game was played. And there was another jingle I recall— but what game it was I can't remember:

> One, two, three, four, five
> Once I caught a little fish alive.

Six, seven, eight, nine, ten
Then I let it go again.
Why did I let him go?
Because he hurt my finger so.
Which finger did it bite?
The little finger on the right.

And here is a jingle from my childhood days which girls used:

Hoxton boys are very nice boys.
Peckham boys are better
But Walworth boys are best of all,
Better, better, better—and *Best*!

at 'Best' they'd dash off to touch their best boy.

'Penny for the Guy' had nothing to do with fireworks or even with Guy Fawkes. Girls played this game. Six large rings were drawn on the ground in some sort of circle. A girl stood on each circle. There was a girl in the centre. She had a school hat in her hands as she said: 'Have you got a penny for my Guy?' 'No,' said a girl in one of the rings, 'but I will see if my neighbour has a penny to spare.' And on the word 'spare' the two girls in circles changed places and the girl in the centre had to get into one of the circles before either girl had completely moved from their circles. If she succeeded then the girl who had lost her circle had to go into the centre, and the game started again. There were at least four feet between each circle, but the girl in the centre had to be very speedy in order to run into a ring before the others had changed places. This game had a variation. The girls sometimes said 'Have you got a match to light my lamp?' and their answer would be 'No—but I'll ask the girl next door'. And the instant 'door' was said they had to change places. Not knowing for sure the *exact* wording of the reply gave a slightly even chance for the girl in the centre. Because one girl could say, 'No—but I will pop across and see if my neighbour has a match.' Action started on the completion of the reply.

'Snakes' was a boys' and girls' game that had to be played within a certain limited area or it would last for hours. A leader would be chosen. Any number of children could play but it seldom exceeded ten. The leader had to chase and touch any of the other nine. Then the leader and first caught held hands tightly and had to run together to catch someone else, and the next one caught held hands with the first two. It became great fun when eight children had to catch the last one. The last one did *not* become the leader. It was the first caught who became the new leader. It was called 'Snakes' because they looked like a frisky snake as they all ran around together tightly holding hands. Anyone who broke the line of gripping hands was out of the game.

'Follow the leader' was another name for this game forty years ago; but I understand that 'Follow the leader' today is a very rough game. If the leader today breaks a window with a brick you break the same window with another brick. And that reminds me that children yesteryear got a lot of fun tying together the knockers of two front doors next to each other. Then they'd bang at one door and rush across the road and watch. As the people in one house came and opened their door the knocker next door would bang as well! Such fun—unless you got caught. It was usually played on foggy nights to enable you to run into the fog and vanish just after the second knocker was banging. Of course you had to hear them and see the residents come out, see them gaze up and down the road, untie the string attached to the next house or explain to the neighbour 'It was kids playing their blooming games'. The fun and the thrill was seeing the annoyance. Another trick was to stick a match-stick into a bell push on a door and start it ringing, then retire to a safe distance to await results.

Nowadays we get so tired in October and November saying 'No' to children begging money—'A penny for the Guy'. It has become almost a racket. Sixty years ago children made grottoes from grass, flowers, bits of glass, cigarette cards and bits of fancy paper, and begged for pennies for the Grotto. I've not seen a grotto for at least twenty years in Southwark. An old resident told me that around 1910–15 grottoes were made of flowers and fancy paper which surrounded the photograph of a dead father or someone close to the child, and it was an understood thing that you gave a penny to help pay for a wreath.

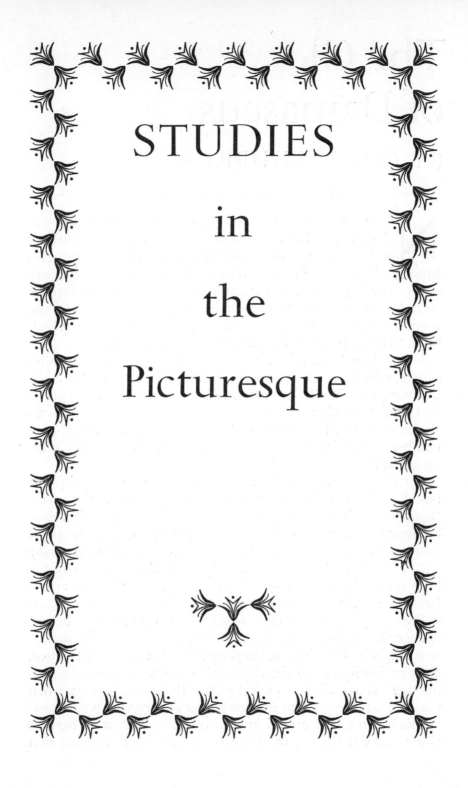

STUDIES

in

the

Picturesque

The Glory
of Damascus

BY COLIN THUBRON

NOW AND AGAIN, by a chance of history, some hitherto obscure city flowers so dramatically into its distinctive genius as to symbolise a whole way of life or thought. Athens, Alexandria, Agra, Florence, Isfahan—the great ages are always fleeting. Then, as each miracle of walls and palaces is sacked, impoverished or ennervated, the city enters into the world's imagination and the spirit outgrows the body, which is left to be haunted and sometimes burdened by it.

Settled in a flood of orchards a hundred and seventy miles square, where the Barada river is loosed from the hills of Anti-Lebanon, the site of Damascus, as her people say, was chosen by God for paradise. It was chosen, too, by the early Moslems as the capital of an empire which became wider than Rome's had been, reaching from the Atlantic to the borders of China, varied, ancient, and dazzlingly rich.

The Damascenes regard their home with affection and pride, but also with the frustration which most Arabs feel for everything which is old, and therefore out-of-date, and therefore backward. The passion for the old belongs chiefly to those surrounded by modernity. The Damascenes have lived too long with history; and over the last fifty years the ancient city has been locked in suburbs which sprawl through the orchards—factories built in paradise: cement, chemical and metallurgical industries, glass and metal, textiles and rubber. But to the stranger it is the old, proud heart which matters, not the shabby new body which encloses it. His perspective, being more detached, gives pride of place to the city's difference, its greatness, which belonged above all to a period of less than ninety years when the Arab empire stood at its zenith, and Europe was in darkness.

This is the oldest capital in the world. Its origins go back to Chalcolithic man, and the Damascenes are fond of saying that

God made Adam from the clay of the Barada river. Certainly the city was ancient when Abraham came, and when the Aramemeans made it head of their kingdom thirteen centuries before Christ. In the time of St Paul, who was cured of blindness there, it was still a wealthy commercial centre. The Romans honoured it with a gigantic temple to Jupiter-Haddad; the Byzantines filled it with their pale-stoned churches; and when the Moslems erupted out of the south in one of the periodic explosions of Semitic peoples into Syria, they saw, as they travelled westward through the desert, a walled and many-gated city set in gardens, which answered to the Prophet's description of Eden: 'This is the paradise which the righteous have been promised; there shall flow in it rivers of unpolluted water.'

The Arabs took the city in A.D. 635, and found themselves rulers of a sophisticated Byzantine middle class and a timeless, suffering peasantry. Mahomet was dead, and for some twenty-five years the caliphate (the word 'caliph' simply meant 'successor') rested in the hands of the austere and simple men in Mecca who had been his close companions. But soon a peculiar situation developed. There flared up again the ancient feud between the two great aristocratic tribes of the Koreish—the Ommayad and the Hashimite, the clan of Mahomet; and when Ali, the fourth caliph and the Prophet's cousin, was murdered on his way to public prayer the path was open for the powerful Ommayad governor of Damascus, Moawiyah, to proclaim himself successor.

So began the city's golden age. The empire's centre of gravity switched from Arabia and Iraq to Syria. The Hashimites gave way to the Ommayads, who had been among the last to accept Islam; and within living memory of the Prophet, who had invoked his followers to prayer and simplicity, the empire of the Faithful was ruled by as sceptical, pleasure-loving a dynasty as there has ever been.

How to write of these dazzling and eccentric rulers? The histories which remain were compiled by their enemies, and are drowned in bias. But clearly Moawiyah I, as the governor of Damascus became, possessed typically Ommayad qualities. He was extraordinarily capable, a cynic, and a master of what the Arabs call *hilm*—a calm, subtle and almost instinctual statecraft. 'I apply not my sword, where my lash suffices,' he declared, 'nor my lash, where my tongue is enough. And even if there be but one hair binding me to my fellow-men, I do not let it break. When they pull, I loosen; and if they loosen, I pull.'

The court at Damascus was sharpened by irreverence and lampoon. His friends taunted him about his name, which meant 'a barking bitch', and jested at his large buttocks. But the caliph could afford to smile at them. In the twenty years of his reign the empire was organised and enriched; it swallowed Persia and edged across North Africa, while the Byzantine fleets were chased to Constantinople. Of Damascus itself little is known at this time, but already the earlier population must have been passing its classical heritage to the Arabs—above all in science, medicine and philosophy. Eighty years later this gift was inherited by the Baghdad caliphate from the Syrian one, and was to be annotated, embellished, and sometimes improved in Islam, and finally given back to Europe through Spain in the dawn of the Renaissance.

If Moawiyah typified Ommayad cunning, his son and successor Yezid I, displayed the family laxity. His mother was a Christian Bedouin, whom Moawiyah had divorced for writing insolent verses, and Yezid had been reared in the desert. Ommayad sympathies had always lain with the nomad more than with the townsman, and it became the custom for the young princes of Damascus to be brought up in the wilds. Later they built pleasure-castles there, which still stand, and grew to love hunting. At every opportunity they abandoned their green-paved palace in the capital and disappeared into the sands for weeks at a time. Half the royal court, with silken tents and an army of servants behind it, might be seen riding through the city into the waste-land. Beside them their salukis pranced, feet bangled in gold; falcons stooped from their wrists; and at the croup of the caliph's saddle, vain as a king, rode his supple and priceless cheetah.

In the chase the salukis, their colour blended to the sand, slipped over the ground almost invisibly, and behind them the half-Bedouin rulers of the greatest empire in the world galloped wildly over the stone-speckled ground, their robes and hair streaming behind them, until the gazelle grew tired from its endless jinking to avoid the falcon's strike, and fell into the jaws of the dogs.

Yezid preferred that the government take care of itself. In Damascus he enjoyed music and poetry rather than administration. And he liked drinking, although the Koran forbade it. He became known as 'Yezid of the Wines'. His favourite drinking-companion was a monkey called Abu Qais, whom he declared to be an old Jew metamorphosed for his sins. It followed the caliph everywhere, dressed as a divine to irritate his religious ministers, and Yezid claimed that its conversation was more interesting than that of his friends.

> My drinking-companion is Abu Qais, for he is ingenious and intelligent
>   When the wit of the company stands mute.

Most of the Ommayad caliphs copied Yezid's drinking in their more regulated ways. Some were continually inebriated. The fourth caliph restricted himself scrupulously to once a month, then took an emetic. His son drank every other day, and Hisham, a puritanical ruler, regulated himself to once a week 'after the divine service'.

But in Yezid's empire the situation was less happy. Ali's youngest son, Husain, rebelled in Iraq and was killed at the battle of Kerbela. To this day the memory of Kerbela rouses to fury the great dissenting sect of Islam, the Shia, who still claim the descendants of Ali as the true heirs of the Prophet. Yezid, with the tolerance of almost all his family, is said to have wept when his generals brought him the head of Husain, and cried out: 'Ill-luck to you! I should have been pleased with your obedience without the murder of al-Husain. . . .'

The Shia were to take a full revenge, but that time was not yet. Soon the empire was at its zenith under the caliphate of Walid. He, say the chroniclers, was 'short in stature with a running nose, proud and self-conceited in his gait', yet he has been called the greatest of the Damascus caliphs, who 'gave every lame person a servant and every blind person a leader'.

He did everything on a grand scale, and it is for this that the Damascenes love him. Moreover he built the Great Mosque,

which still stands. Look around the city now for the remnants of
its golden age, and you will always be returned to this. Nothing
like it remains. It is the city's glory, and, after Mecca, Medinah
and Jerusalem, is the holiest place in Islam. Built where the
Byzantines had dedicated a church to St John, where the Romans before them had raised a temple to Jupiter, and where the
Arameans had worshipped Haddad for a thousand years before
that, the mosque was grafted on to the existing walls, which
are the superb work of Rome. Thirty-foot columns still frame
its entranceway, and all around it, muddled in with bazaars on
one side and the tomb of Saladin on the other, the classical
pillars are propped and strewn.

Twelve thousand craftsmen, said the historians (who invent
their figures), were brought from Byzantium. More came from
Egypt, and perhaps even from Persia, India and West Africa.
And when the people complained of Walid's extravagance he
emptied the contents of the treasury into the mosque to prove
the wealth of the empire; and the mountain of riches, enough
for three years' state expenditure, was so high that it divided one
half of the building from the other.

In the end he spent seven years' income on the mosque, with
many shiploads of gold and silver from Cyprus. The accounts
were brought to him piled on eighteen camels, and he refused to
read them, saying, 'Verily we have spent this for God and we
will make no account of it.'

The mosque was largely the work of Byzantines and Christian
Syrians. The architects were Greek. Even its form—a long hall
built along one side of the Roman courtyard—followed the
three-aisled pattern of a contemporary church, and glittered
with mosaics lit by six hundred lamps dangling from golden
chains. The courtyard walls were panelled inside with veined
marble for twice the height of a man. Ancient columns were
commandeered for the porticos, and still bear Greek dedica-
tions: 'In accordance with his will, the inheritors of N. . . .'
'After the will of Zenon, son of Diodore, son of Metrodore.'

It is hard to divine what qualities the Arabs themselves brought
to this mish-mash of Christian and classical; but the marble
grilles and gold-gilt capitals, the intricate and magnificent

mihrab—the niche which points to Mecca, the mosaics from which all saints and gods were banished, and the sepulchral marble which paved the courtyard for some sixty thousand square yards, must have lent the sanctuary a half-barbaric, half-fastidious splendour for whose synthesis the Arab was responsible.

The Moslems, in their eclectic way, sanctioned much in Christian tradition. They declared that St George came every night to the mosque to pray, and that on the last day Christ would descend upon the south-eastern minaret, the Pinnacle of Jesus, would judge the dead and send the Christians, as well as the Jews, to hell. Stranger still, there stands near the centre of the prayer-hall a vulgar Baroque catafalque which is said to enshrine the head of John the Baptist. The Moslems have a weakness for him. They say his head was sent by Herod to the Roman proconsul in Damascus, and that it was buried here in a silver coffer. Certainly the Christians in the fourth century consecrated the site to St John, but the earliest reference to the head itself seems to come from medieval writers. They declared that during the construction of the mosque, when the Church of St John was destroyed, a cave was discovered beneath it. That night Walid descended into the cave in secret with candle-bearers, and found, locked in three shrines and enclosed in a silver casket, the head of the Baptist 'still covered with skin and hair, without the least change'.

But what is left now of the Great Mosque after twelve centuries? The tourist, shod in a pair of outsize but compulsory slippers, is ushered with misgiving into the courtyard. He finds the marble mostly stripped, the arcades thickened by piers, the gold gone, the prayer-hall rebuilt. Yet inside the ghost of Roman walls the courtyard still spreads, in pale limestone now, indomitably old and suffering. It seems to be consecrated less to Allah than to silence, to age, and to the whole pantheon of gods which has sanctified the place. It is bounded on three sides by honey-coloured colonnades, fifty feet high. The medieval Minaret of the Bride is still there, refurbished, from which beacons were relayed to Cairo to tell of Mongols crossing the Euphrates. Here and there, too, is a fragment of Ommayad veined marble, an inscribed column.

But one work especially—of a beauty and originality which place it among the finest in Islam and in the world—has been spared. Under a part of the western colonnade, high and perfect as when Walid commissioned it, is a section of the mosaic which once banded the inside of the courtyard walls for twenty thousand square feet—the largest ever executed. It is the colours, at a glance, which are most striking: a compound of gold and green which at once suggests Mahomet's paradise. Along the foot of the mosaic runs a river whose course unites the composittion. It is vivid blue, except where tiny wateralls break it in white claws. Along its banks superb trees rise. Their smooth boles flower into a yellow-green richness of leaves and fruit, and behind them the sky shimmers fiercely gold from the Byzantine habit of inclining the *tesserae* at an angle of thirty-five degrees from the plaster. Between them a scene of phantasmal palaces and pavilions unfolds: pleasure-domes in whose arcades glint lanterns made of mother of pearl. It is a childlike dream, a fairy-tale but realised with such minuteness that one wonders if such a fantasy was not, after all, copied from some original, if anything so halcyon could have existed.

On closer inspection the architectural elements begin to resolve themselves. One notices Corinthian columns, the cockleshell niche common to Byzantine churches, and in villages climbing steeply among rocks the defensive windows and pent roofs of early Syrian houses. Scholars have found here the wraiths of Pompeiian-style frescoes, Chinese temples, Ptolemaic pavilions. But each element climbs on the shoulders of the next in a perspective which follows its own harmonious law, and tapers to the glistening sky in a tented roof or a sheaf of columns. Its strangeness is due in part to there being no people to inhabit this paradise—such representation may have been forbidden to Moslems even at this time. So the mansions stand on the blue river untenanted for ever, and the gold-green vision, acknowledged as the most beautiful mosaic of its kind, remains alien and mysterious as the landscape of innocence will always be.

During the reign of Walid, Damascus—like the empire itself— touched its meridian. Moslem armies sacked Samarkand,

The medieval Minaret of the Bride

conquered Afghanistan, and planted the white banner of the Ommayads on the edge of China. And from the west, as a crowning triumph, were brought four hundred of the yellow-haired Visigothic royalty of Spain, who knelt before Walid in the Great Mosque with the captured altar of Toledo Cathedral.

The city itself became increasingly Arab. The Christians and Jews were tolerated, and still formed the pith of the civil service, but the Moslem was aristocrat, ruler and general. Arabic superseded Greek as the language of government. The first permanent Islamic mint was founded. A prodigious slave-market developed. Yet a desert freedom still pervaded the newcomers. There were none of the oriental prostrations and servility which stultified the later, Persia-orientated court in Baghdad. Eunuchs and extensive harems were almost unknown except in Byzantium, and women, although they veiled in public, aspired to more freedom and dignity than they were to know for more than a thousand years after. The Ommayad princesses were frequently formidable in their homes; one of them even owned a stable and took part in horse-racing.

Nevertheless, the royal life of Damascus was insensibly growing grander and more pompous. At audiences the caliph sat cross-legged on golden cushions, backed by his ministers and secretaries in ceremonial robes specially woven in Egypt, while on his right his paternal relatives, and on his left his maternal ones, dressed in radiant silks, must have constituted as splendid a gallery of ability, cunning and debauchery as ever graced a court in Islam. But the arts which the Ommayads favoured were still those of the pagan desert, of which Mahomet had been suspicious: singing, dance and poetry. Poetry in particular retained its nomad force for many years before succumbing to a mannered flattery. The Ommayad armies recited round their camp-fires. Their generals composed. Their courtiers slandered one another in verse; and several of the caliphs were poets.

The rulers who followed Walid were mostly cast in one or other of the familiar family types: subtle and capable, or hopelessly lax and indulgent. Only Omar II, pious and ascetic, strikes a discordant, faintly priggish note. And his relatives, of course, poisoned him. Before him ruled a more typical Ommayad, Sulei-

The northern portico of the Great Mosque

man, who died of indigestion after eating seventy pomegranates, a lamb, six fowls and an unspecified poundage of currants; he had such a passion for silks that he asked to be buried in them.

Then came Yezid II, who cared only for his slave-girl, whom he mistakenly choked by playfully throwing a pomegranate seed into her mouth. For three days he clung to her, 'until she began to stink, when he ordered her to be buried'; but even so he had her disinterred, and himself died of grief a few days later. More outrageous still was Walid II, who retired to his desert palace where visitors recounted how he swooned away with ecstasy when listening to songs, and bathed in a swimming-pool of wine. His atheism was so blatant that he sent a drunken concubine to lead the faithful at the Friday prayer, and planned an orgy on the roof of the Holy Kaaba.

But the Ommayad day was over. Soon after Walid's murder a sect which had chosen as its leader a descendant of Abbas, Mahomet's uncle, set up its black standard in Khorasan. All over the empire the Abbasids and Shia rebelled. In Persia and Iraq the Syrian garrisons were annihilated, and even the Yemenites defected. When the black and white banners met at last in a decisive battle near the Tigris the Ommayad power was broken. The last caliph was surrounded in a Coptic church, and died breathing 'Now is our dynasty passed!'; and Damascus, captured in 750, dwindled to the status of a provincial capital. Only one of the royal lineage is known to have survived, and he fled to Spain and perpetuated the Ommayad name there in the glorious kingdom of Cordoba.

Even the Ommayad graves were defiled by the puritan fury of their enemies, but their bodies had already mostly decomposed. There is a rumour, nevertheless, that the tomb of Moawiyah remains. After wandering down many alleys—so narrow that a donkey is the only transport there, as is the way with Damascus streets—the enquirer is shown a domed mausoleum, piled with rubbish. Inside it is a ridge of baked clay, a grave as humble as a peasant's, and the awe-filled voice of the guide says: 'That is the tomb of Moawiyah, the great king!' Yet certainly it is not, for the historians agree that he was buried in the Bab Saghir cemetery, which stretches like a field of marble south of the city, outside the entrance which the Romans called the Gate of Mars. Here the keeper shows a clay hut. Inside is a heavy, limestone sarcophagus, and beside this is the bed of the keeper himself, who is convinced that he sleeps by the side of the first Damascus caliph.

For years there was a tradition that Yezid of the Wines was buried in the cemetery too. The Shia would make a pilgrimage of hate to the graveyard, to throw rocks at his tomb. Eventually this cracked and disintegrated, and was marked only by their heaps of stones. When these were recently cleared away, there was nothing at all to be seen.

The Ommayad caliphs reigned for some ninety years, but have left little to Damascus but the fragmentary vision of paradise on the walls of the Great Mosque; and the ordinary Damascene regards them almost as myths, who belonged to a time when Syria was great, and not the plaything of petty politicians and generals.

Yet the people of Damascus themselves, compared with those of other Middle Eastern towns, have inherited an aristocracy of manner which is perhaps the heirloom of a city that was once the world's capital. Among other Arabs they are famous for their love of good living, their elaborate politeness, their grace and musicality. Moreover, they are gourmets, and are exceedingly vain about clothes. It is no doubt foolish to see these qualities as a legacy from their sybaritic heyday, and certainly the old tolerance is gone. But one day, they half playfully assert, when they come into their own again, it will be a mystic scion of the house of Ommaya who will plant his white banner on the crumbling walls, and lead his city to an age of pride and peace.

The Assembly Rooms at Bath

BY V. C. CHAMBERLAIN

DRAWINGS BY MICHAEL FELMINGHAM

O N SEPTEMBER 30, 1771, the New, or Upper, Assembly Rooms in the City of Bath opened with a grand Ridotto, or Ball. Completely restored twice in their chequered career, these Rooms are probably the finest suite of their kind in Britain or indeed anywhere in the world.

In the second half of the eighteenth century the Georgian City of Bath was developing rapidly northwards, up the steep slopes of Lansdown and along the London Road—the New, or Upper Town which was growing up under the influence of the younger John Wood, the local architect. To meet the social needs of the ever-increasing number of visitors to the City, and, a newer factor, the ever-increasing number of permanent or semi-permanent residents, there arose a demand for a new suite of Rooms. The two Rooms in the centre of the City, near the Abbey, over which the famous Master of Ceremonies, Beau Nash, had reigned for so many years, were inadequate.

Various schemes were put forward for the new Rooms. Robert Adam, the famous architect who at the time was devising the layout of the Pulteney estate in the City, submitted an elaborate competitive design, now preserved in the Soane Museum in London. In the end a more modest scheme by the younger John Wood, who had just completed his famous Royal Crescent, was accepted by the promoters, and 'the most noble and elegant Assembly Rooms of any in the Kingdom' were quickly completed, just off the well-known Circus, at a cost of some £20,000. The foundation stone had been laid by Wood on May 24, 1769, when 'a band of music attended, and great ceremony was observed', followed by cakes and wine.

Among the original subscribers to the scheme, which was on

the tontine principle, very common in those days, were James Leigh Perrot (uncle of Jane Austen), William Hoare (the Bath portrait painter), his brother, Prince Hoare the sculptor, Walter Wiltshire (friend and patron of Gainsborough and proprietor of one of the Lower Rooms already referred to), Thomas Bowdler (the original 'bowdleriser'), many prominent local citizens, and the architect John Wood himself.

The New Rooms were arranged to a simple U-plan, with excellent accommodation for carriages and sedan chairs, with easy access to the streets and protection from the elements. There was a large Ballroom, some one hundred feet by forty, a Tea Room, some sixty feet by forty, and a Card or Concert Room, the Great Octagon, some forty-eight feet in diameter. There were magnificent chandeliers by Jonathan Collett and William Parker, of London. At the outset there was some chandelier trouble. Those by Collett in the Ballroom proved to be unsafe, and were soon taken down and replaced by Parker. To

compensate for this loss Collett made a magnificent chandelier for the centre of the Great Octagon.

Later on, to meet the ever-increasing demands for accommodation, a Coffee Room and an additional Card Room—the one made famous by Mr Pickwick—were added, together with facilities for billiards and reading. An unusual feature, in this type of building, was a small circular plunge bath, under the Ballroom.

The opening Ridotto was advertised far and wide—in the Bath, Bristol and Salisbury newspapers, and in the *London Evening Post*, and the *Public Advertiser*. The doors were to be open at seven, the side-boards at nine, and the shut-down was to be at twelve. Tickets for one gentleman and two ladies were one guinea; single tickets for gentlemen were half a guinea, and for ladies were seven shillings. The receipts amounted to £281 15s.

Among the guests were young Richard Brinsley Sheridan, whose family were frequent visitors, and the lovely Elizabeth Linley, the Bath singer with whom he was soon to elope from the new Linley home in the fashionable Royal Crescent.

Elizabeth's father, Thomas Linley, the well-known Bath musician, directed the music. His orchestra of ten included Alexander Herschel, the 'cellist, brother of the famous astronomer William Herschel, who was originally an organist at the Octagon Chapel, Milson Street, Bath.

Sheridan wrote a poem vividly describing the scene, *The Ridotto of Bath—a Panegyrick*, which was first published in the *Bath Chronicle*. The chandeliers had caught his eye.

> Both splendidly lit with new chandeliers,
> With drops hanging down like the bobs at *Peg's* ears;
> While jewels of *paste* reflected the rays,
> And *Bristol-stone* diamonds gave strength to the blaze:
> So that it was doubtful, to view the bright clusters,
> Which sent the most light, the ear-rings or lustres.

Summing up the general tone, he wrote:

> The motley assemblage, so blended together,
> 'Twas mob, or Ridotto—'twas both, or 'twas neither.

For the next half-century and more the New Rooms were the scene of some of the most brilliant balls and concerts held anywhere in England. Intense competition among the supporters of the different Rooms in the City sometimes took a bizarre form, such as the wearing of an extremely high coiffure, surmounted by feathers! There was a particularly magnificent Ball in 1775 in honour of the young Duke of Cumberland and his pretty wife, Anne, who was said to have the most amorous eyes in the world and eyelashes a yard long! This Ball was so successful that the Duke patronised a special New Year Ball two years later.

In 1774 Dr Johnson, Mrs Thrale, Boswell, and party visited the Rooms, and Boswell was 'giddy with the sight'. In 1779 Admiral Keppel received his 'home-made laurels' at a public breakfast in the Tea Room, a reception about which that Queen of the Blue-stockings, Mrs Elizabeth Montagu, was satirical.

In 1796 a Ball was graced by the First Gentleman in Europe, the then Prince of Wales, and his brother, the Duke of York, who was quite a frequent visitor. The last Ball patronised by royalty

The Tea Room

was held in 1801, when, by command of the Duchess of York, an even more frequent visitor than the Duke, a special Ball was given in aid of the widows and orphans of men who had lost their lives before the walls of Copenhagen. Nelson's father, a frequent visitor, was present. In 1817 Queen Charlotte, who was in Bath for her health, visited the Rooms, in her red cloak and pattens. It was a surprise visit.

As Hannah More, the West Country Blue-stocking and writer, and a frequent visitor and later resident, put it, from personal observation, 'Princes and kings that will be, and princes and kings that have been, pop upon you at every corner.'

On the musical side, under the able leadership of the Italian musician Venanzio Rauzzini, after Thomas Linley had left the City for London, visitors to the New Rooms heard some of the finest music of the day. It is also interesting to note that Bath was one of the first cities to have a civic orchestra.

In time, however, for a variety of inevitable reasons, the social life of Bath, which had been so adroitly and skilfully nurtured, first by Beau Nash, and later by Captain Wade, ran out of steam. A remarkable period of our social history had run its course. We know from Jane Austen's *Persuasion*, set in the year after Waterloo, that the New Rooms were not fashionable enough for the Elliots, who, like many others at that time, were more given to the private party. She herself had found the last Ball of the season, in May 1801, a dull affair.

By the eighteen-thirties, when Mr Pickwick played his immortal game of cards in the New Rooms, with the Dowager Lady Snuphanuph, Mrs Colonel Wugsby and Miss Bolo, the latter eventually going straight home in a flood of tears and a sedan chair, the general atmosphere was one of somewhat boring gentility and snobbery, rather than the exuberant gaiety originally intended. By this time, too, both the Lower Rooms had disappeared. One was demolished in 1794, and the other, soon after the 'grand fête' there of Dr Johnson's friend, Mrs Piozzi, in 1820, was burnt down.

Throughout the Victorian period the New Rooms were usually as dull as the average drawing-room at that time. There were, however, occasional highlights. Excellent music continued, and from time to time there was the outstanding ball, play or reading. Dickens was frequently there, acting or reading. Fanny Kemble read there. In 1851, in the Ballroom, Dickens and his band of theatricals performed Bulwer Lytton's farce *Not So Bad as We Seem*, to a packed and fashionable audience. The cast included Douglas Jerrold, John Forster, Mark Lemon, F. W. Topham, Peter Cunningham, Charles Knight, Wilkie Collins, John Tenniel, Frank Stone and Dudley Costello.

Early in the present century, however, things went from bad to worse. The Rooms became, in turn, a factory, an Army mess, a cinema, an exhibition hall. Eventually many of the valuables were sold, including the portrait of Captain Wade, which passed into the ownership of the then Lord Burton, of Rangemore, Burton-on-Trent, the well-known brewer. This fine picture now hangs in a prominent place in Birmingham Art Gallery, by kind permission of the present Lord Burton.

Early in the 'thirties, however, the tide began to turn. A then anonymous donor, Mr E. E. Cook, the connoisseur and collector, who lived in the City, made it possible for the Society for the Protection of Ancient Buildings to secure the Rooms, and they were eventually placed under the care of the National Trust, which in turn leased them to the Bath Corporation. Fully restored to their former magnificence the Rooms were re-opened in 1938 by the then Duchess of Kent.

The new life of gaiety and splendour was very short-lived, however. Early in World War Two the Rooms were completely gutted by fire—the victim of the Baedeker raids in 1942. Only the shell remained. Luckily the chandeliers had been stored.

Twenty-five years afterwards, in 1963, once again fully and sensitively restored, the Rooms were re-opened by the same Duchess. Since then the Bath Corporation have done their very best to make the Rooms a cultural and social centre. They house a Museum of Costume, based on Mrs Langley Moore's well-known collection. The new university holds important functions there. Above all, however, the Rooms remain, as they were two hundred years ago, when Philip Thicknesse, that outspoken critic of the time, pronounced them the FIRST of the kind in *Europe*, the most festive and magnificent in Britain.

Chalk, Rocks & Shells

BY MONICA POOLE

NINETY MILLION YEARS ago chalk was being formed by
the tiny coccoliths. Microscopic plants, the skeletons of
which fell to the sea bed and fossilised, made the soft
white rock, building perhaps an inch in a thousand years. It
has taken a much shorter time for the sea to wear away the coast;
to leave the tall cliffs standing and to mould and smooth the
rocks at their feet to these curious, greyish shapes. At every
tide the sand twists itself into new patterns and the lumps of
loose chalk, rounded by the water and of their true whiteness,
re-dispose themselves.

Flints and mussel shells form dark clusters against the light
rock, itself pitted and scarred by limpets and winkles. The pools
are alive; crabs conceal themselves in the sand, little shrimps
dart, and the soft, purplish blobs of the sea anemone flower as
the water covers them.

134

SHELLS have a unique magic left over from childhood. Marvellous in design and colour, we find them at our feet on the sand and may pick them up and possess them. Indeed it seems almost a duty to take the delicate objects from the beach to save them from destruction by the heavy waves which so unaccountably placed them there without damage. At home they take their place as treasures with the snail shells from the chalk land and the fossils of the sponge and sea-urchin.

135

IN THE CREVICES of the rocks pebbles, shells and flints collect. Holes are bored in the soft chalk by the little piddock, and broken shells reveal more of their precise and complicated structure. The black flints break and are sometimes found lightened by exposure. These distinctively shaped objects, so hard that the sea does little to round their sharp broken edges, are the soft in-fillings of crustacean burrows subsequently converted to this quartz-like substance.

136

WHERE the cleft leads from one part of the old quarry to another the chalk is loosely packed, and grey and smoothed a little by time. Uneven projections on the face remind us of the moment when men laid down their picks many years ago. On the quarry floor little birch trees grow in the rubble, and boulders falling from the rock face split into thin, sharp-edged shapes, perfectly white.

IN THE LATER PART of the quarry we find the patterns made
by the claws of the excavator which superseded the pick.
Here one sees the horizontal cracks in the cliff where the
depositing of the sediment which formed the chalk was per-
iodically interrupted. Here frost has split the grey boulders lying
at the bottom of the steep scree which carries down with it the
twisted roots of bushes from the quarry's edge.

Costa Blanca

BY JOHN BETJEMAN

SHE:

THE COSTA BLANCA! Skies without a stain!
    Eric and I at almond-blossom time
    Came here and fell in love with it. The climb
Under the pine trees up the dusty lane
To *Casa Kenilworth* brought back again
    Our honeymoon when I was in my prime.
    Goodbye 'democracy' and smoke and grime,
Eric retires next year. We're off to Spain.

We've found the perfect site beside the shore
    Owned by a charming Spaniard, Miguel,
    Who says that he is quite prepared to sell
And build our Casa for us, and, what's more,
    Preposterously cheaply. I have found
    Delightful English people living round.

HE:

Mind if I see your *Times*? We used to share
    Our *Telegraph* with people who've returned—
    And there's another bloody thing I've learned,
If you come out here put aside the fare
For getting home again. We're caught all right:
There wasn't any water on the site
    Renée was talked into by Miguel.
    Bang went our savings, and my pension's—well . . .
In Spain the winter's bloody cold at night.

Too many 'bloodys' are there in my talk?
    And so there'd be in yours, if you were me,
    Wrecked on this tideless, tourist-ridden sea,
Year in year out. Renée and I must walk
    Longing for England down a stinking path
    Back to our flat with scorpions in the bath.

PHOTOGRAPH BY LORD ROSSMORE

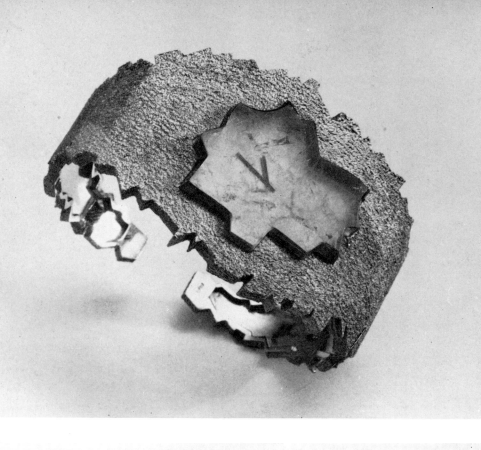

Watches as Jewels

BY ANNA MOTSON

PHOTOGRAPHS BY FRANK GRIMA

A WATCH is a functional object, created to fulfil a practical need. This perhaps explains why it has been neglected by the world's best designers of jewelry. A watch has always been looked upon as a piece of machinery rather than a piece of jewelry. The rapid advance in technology increased this feeling even more, as greater and greater degrees of time-keeping accuracy became possible. The watch as a machine was refined far beyond everyday human needs.

Eventually someone thought of turning it into a fashion accessory, and before long the market was swamped with cheap, trendy wristwatches with garish faces and lollipop-coloured straps. They became the new status symbol. At this point traditional watch makers like Omega in Switzerland began to get worried. Now that the watch had ceased to be a purely functional object, accuracy was no longer enough. The industry needed to be revitalised, but who could do it? In an unprecedented move, Omega approached one of Britain's top jewelry designers, Andrew Grima, and invited him to create a collection of time-pieces around Omega movements. He could have a completely free hand in terms of materials and cost. Grima, who had never designed a watch before, found the challenge irresistible.

In order to understand why Swiss Omega, established for over a hundred years, should look outside their own country for the first time, and then to a man whose work had never

Opposite above: 'Greenland' features an irregularly cut pink tourmaline 'glass'. A hand-sawn gold-bangle echoes the shape of the stone.

Below: 'Haze' has a high, smoky quartz 'glass' cut in a block shape. Its rich colour is set off by a square wedge of diamonds at the base.

included watch design, one must first understand something about Andrew Grima. He was born in Rome, of an Italian mother and a Maltese father, the first of their seven children. When he was five years old the Grima family moved to England, where his artistic gifts were soon apparent. As a young boy he would set off alone in the early light of dawn with a sketch pad, sometimes walking many miles before returning at dusk with the pad completely filled. Even as a boy he felt instinctively that his future lay in designing, without having any clear idea of the medium through which he could best express himself. It was pure chance that it should turn out to be jewelry. Soon after the war he married a jeweller's daughter, and when his father-in-law died in 1951 the business passed into his hands.

He inherited more than just a workshop; he inherited a tradition of taste and design with which he soon realised he had little sympathy. A piece of jewelry was primarily a sign of wealth for the wearer, an investment for the buyer. The important thing was the value of the stones, and little or no consideration was given therefore to the design.

As an artist, Grima found this unacceptable. He began to move away from traditional forms by applying basic principles of art to jewelry design. He began, in fact, to sketch in gold and precious stones. Shapes became abstract, goldwork more imaginative, precious stones larger and more important. The challenge of making a large stone look elegant rather than overpowering was something that captured Grima's imagination from the very beginning, and though his style has developed considerably since then, elegance and bold design have remained constant features of his work.

But conservatism runs deep, and conservatism in taste is particularly difficult to overcome. Finding an outlet for the first designs from the new-style Grima workshop turned out to be far from easy. London jewellers were sceptical, and fought shy of taking a risk with work that was so unconventional. Provincial shopkeepers were even less interested; so Grima packed his bags and set off for the Continent. Here his work aroused considerable interest, and his complete collection was sold within weeks. Further afield, in the United States and

Australia, the welcome was even warmer. Recognition on an international scale followed soon afterwards. In 1965 Grima won five Diamond International Awards—the 'Oscars' of the jewelry world—and in 1966, his most triumphant year, he won the Queen's Award to Industry, followed by the Duke of Edinburgh's Prize for Elegant Design. Since then he has gone on to win six more Diamond International Awards, more than any other entrant, and in 1970 he was granted the Royal Warrant.

The fact that Grima's designs are now popular as well as professional is evident from the success of his own London shop, opened in 1966 at 80 Jermyn Street. His continuing success overseas is reflected in the additional shops since established in New York and Sydney.

It was perhaps Grima's gift for combining sophistication with wearability that attracted Omega. In inviting him to turn his talents to watches Omega's enlightened managing director, Robert Forster, knew that he would create a collection above the tides of fashion, a collection that would be a work of art in its own right. But the significance of the Grima collection goes even further. In turning the watch into a jewel Grima hit on a simple yet brilliant idea, the substitution of a precious or semi-precious stone for each watch glass. It is this revolutionary idea of seeing time through stones that not only forms the unifying theme of the 'About Time' collection, but also ensures Andrew Grima his place in the history of the watch.

Surprisingly, the designs themselves were produced in a matter of minutes, not days or weeks as one might expect. Grima is an eternal doodler; he will draw anywhere, on anything, and many of his watch designs were first sketched on restaurant tablecloths or hotel menus. Some of them took less than two minutes to produce, none of them took more than eight.

The complete 'About Time' collection consisted of eighty-six pieces—fifty-five watches and thirty-one matching jewels—all made by hand. The revolutionary nature of the designs meant that stone-cutters were called on to cut precious and semi-precious stones in shapes and sizes that had never before been attempted, and the whole project faced Grima's own craftsmen with the highest test of their skill ever encountered.

The result was a triumph. Outstanding workmanship, reflected in the period of between six weeks and four months taken to complete each piece, transformed Andrew Grima's designs into breathtaking reality. In May 1970, after an intensive year of work and preparation, the 'About Time' collection was launched at an exhibition at Goldsmiths' Hall in London.

If Omega were at all concerned about the reception it would receive, they were soon reassured. The response was overwhelming, not only from the Press but from the public. By the end of the first week more than three thousand people had passed through the exhibition hall, and about half the watches had been sold. Prices were high, between £660 and £7,500, but they have already proved an attractive investment.

The exhibition went straight from London to join Expo '70 in Osaka. It is now travelling the world, and will have been shown in nearly every major city by the end of 1972. As each watch is sold, it is replaced by a new design, which not only keeps the collection up to strength but also retains the uniqueness of each piece. Nearly all the original exhibits have been sold.

The 'About Time' collection is more than just a prestige project. Omega set out to change the attitude of the public towards their wristwatches, and the creation of an exclusive collection was only the first step in this direction. The second step was the adaptation of the new ideas to suit the mass market. This is being achieved by the creation of a so-called Omega/ Grima second generation of watches. These make use of Andrew Grima's central idea of using a semi-precious stone instead of a watch glass, but the watches themselves are produced by the Omega factory instead of being made by hand. This obviously means that they can be offered at a very much lower price, and the first ones, which should be in the shops by Christmas 1971, will be priced at between £250 and £500.

This is perhaps the real significance of Andrew Grima's revolution in watch design. It is one thing to create beauty that can only be available to the select few; it is quite another to achieve this in such a way that it can be made readily available without destroying its artistic essence. To have done this is Andrew Grima's triumph.

Above: 'Linenfold', a perfect rock crystal, surrounded by a skirt of diamonds. The fine lines in the stone are known as rutile needles, a natural phenomenon formed over millions of years. Lines as fine as these are known as 'venus hair'.

Below, left: 'Spring' ring watch. A velvety green peridot 'glass' circled by fine diamonds.

Below, right: An enormous glowing moonstone snaps up to reveal the 'Midnight' watch. The white gold ring is scattered with sapphires.

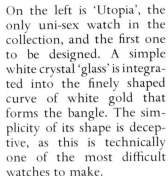

On the left is 'Utopia', the only uni-sex watch in the collection, and the first one to be designed. A simple white crystal 'glass' is integrated into the finely shaped curve of white gold that forms the bangle. The simplicity of its shape is deceptive, as this is technically one of the most difficult watches to make.

On the right: 'Elegance', the watch chosen by Princess Anne. The shape of the smoky quartz stone is echoed by the individual blocks of textured gold forming the bracelet. Notice how the shape of the hands is adapted to complement each design. Here there is a further departure from tradition, as the gold hands are set to one side of the watch face.

On the left is shown 'Enigma', the first of three men's watches in the collection. The simplicity of the sweeping gold triangle is emphasised by a rich green tourmaline 'glass' set deep into the surface. This is the only watch to make a design feature of the winder, which is otherwise concealed

On the right: 'Gondola' bracelet watch, so-called because of the shape of the deeply concave smoky quartz 'glass'. Finely engraved lines in the brushed gold face indicate quarter hours.

'Tornado', above, is one of the heaviest watches in the collection, weighing $\frac{1}{2}$ lb. A rutilated quartz 'glass' is caught in a springy bangle of polished wires. Diamond strips scattered over the surface highlight the intricacy of the goldwork.

'Jigsaw' clip watch, on the left, features a puzzle-shaped piece of gold, polished and set with diamonds. A centre puzzle of pink tourmaline forms the 'glass' and the position of the hands is marked by a single diamond. 'Jigsaw' has a matching set of ear-clips and a ring.

'Firedance', above, is one of several pendant watches in the collection. An unusually cut citrine is surrounded by strong, irregular bars of carved gold. These are thrown into relief by five similar bars set with diamonds. The pendant is completed by a matching chain of linked gold bars.

'Whirlpool' is the name of the clip watch on the right, so-called because of the fluid shape of the unusual citrine 'glass'. The diamond crust is shadowed by an outer edge of brandy-coloured diamonds.

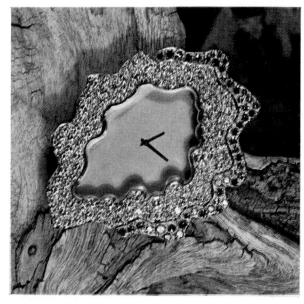

'Alpine,' opposite, is a man's pocket watch of smoky quartz with a matching gold torch.

The 'Armada' pill box, below, on the opposite page, has a fine, smoky quartz lid, and stands one inch high. Alongside it is 'Golden glory', a ring watch. A fine cabochon citrine opens to reveal a minute watch.

On the right is 'Cerini,' a bangle watch of thatched gold, with a bright yellow citrine 'glass'. Below, on this page, is 'Caribbean', Andrew Grima's personal favourite. An irregular aquamarine rock forms part of a supple bracelet of individually linked gold scales. Bright diamonds provide an exciting contrast to the matt, heavily textured gold, and the rich blue aquamarine.

The Art of Smoking

BY J. B. PRIESTLEY

IT IS NOW over sixty years since I first began smoking a pipe. I smoke when I am working, smoke when I am thinking or pretend to myself I am thinking, and rather too often smoke when I am talking. (The point here being that a pipe and a rumbling lazy voice sometimes make me inaudible. But are my hearers missing much? Probably not.) As any good dictionary of quotations will testify, different generations of sensitive and sensible men have regarded tobacco as their friend. But now, in our age of pollution, an enormous attack is being mounted against 'smoking'. *Stop it at once!* we are told.

Now I am not blaming doctors, asked to cure lung cancer or chronic bronchitis, for denouncing 'smoking'. But when they tell me that they themselves have long ago 'stopped smoking' I feel inclined to retort that in fact they never really started smoking. Putting a quick succession of lighted fuses into the mouth and then drawing their fumes deep into the lungs—this is not smoking as I understand and practise it. The enjoyment of tobacco hardly comes into the picture. Most cigarette addicts would continue even if their paper tubes were filled with dried camel dung.

Moreover, while I do not blame the crusading doctors, I must reveal a certain suspicion that troubles me. Some of the more fanatical enemies of tobacco seem to me to be puritans popping up again. They hate it because it gives pleasure. Your genuine puritan always combines with his hatred of pleasure a deep respect for power, business, making money. I remember how a group of New York medical men, when reporting on 'leading executives', denounced their smoking, drinking, hearty dining, but passed over in silence their daily commuting among diesel fumes, the eight telephones on their desks, all the idiotic fuss and worry of intensely competitive commerce.

Three other points are worth making. No doubt I might be healthier without tobacco, but, though health is important, I do not feel I exist in order to be healthy: I try to be a fully creative,

Toby jug by Ralph Wood, *c.* 1770
(Victoria & Albert Museum, London)

hard-working, friendly, tolerant human being. Again, we are angrily denounced for spending so much money on tobacco, when in fact what we are chiefly doing is making a huge contribution to state revenue. If everybody stopped smoking this year, non-smokers would soon be horrified by the new increase in taxation. Finally, we are told that using tobacco is 'a dirty habit'. Well, of course, stupid slovenly people can make anything dirty. But there is nothing particularly dirty about enjoying good tobacco in a clean cool pipe. If we are going to be so wonderfully fastidious, then life itself is a dirty habit—all that eating, drinking sweating, defecating and urinating and procreating—what a messy business! Clearly we ought to exist in sterilised glass cases, waited upon by computers.

Now I must explain why the proper enjoyment of a pipe is quite different from the 'smoking' that is now being attacked and savagely condemned. (And there is such a cry for banning tobacco that I may find myself enjoying my final pipes only in the lavatory.) First, no pipesmoker in his right mind ever inhales. He is not filling his lungs with smoke, hardly filling his mouth. He is gently and rather slowly puffing away. Secondly—and this follows straight on—if he really knows how to enjoy a pipe he is producing no great heat but keeps the tobacco merely smouldering. No burning paper is involved. Tobacco itself does not burn easily, soon going out if not attended to; so I suspect that it is highly combustible paper that makes constant cigarette-smoking a risk.

Certainly I have known a good many pipesmokers who behaved as if they were in charge of a furnace. Often their pipe bowls would be burnt and charred out of shape. This is idiotic smoking, making the worst of the job. Equally idiotic is the man who smokes hard but carries only one pipe with him, so that he is for ever puffing away at a hot pipe and destroying the flavour and fragrance of his tobacco. It is these fellows who give us a bad name. For my part I always carry three pipes, and keep about a dozen on my desk, so I never fill and light a hot pipe. I think I can safely add that even a pipe I had just finished smoking would not be really hot, because I smoke slowly and am not in the furnace business. Good tobacco tastes best and smells best when it is simply smouldering. Here begins the art of smoking.

Almost all the men I have known who tried a pipe but then declared they could not 'get on with it' have made the same two mistakes. They began with pipes that had bowls that were not big enough and were not thick enough. They also began with the wrong kind of tobacco, probably a Light Virginia, finely cut, rather like cigarette tobacco. Puffing away at this bad combination of pipe and tobacco, they would soon find themselves with a very hot smoke indeed, would react by producing a great deal of saliva, would then decide they were 'wet smokers' and have no more to do with a pipe. Whereas if they had tried a bigger and thicker pipe and what they imagined to be a 'stronger tobacco', simply because it looked much darker, then all would soon have been well.

Now a few brief notes on pipes themselves. I have experimented with all kinds, but what we call the Briar* is by far the best. Pipes with patent gadgets in them and pipes made of synthetic substances never seem to me to taste right, so should be avoided. Good pipes are very expensive these days; but, even so, it is false economy to buy cheap pipes. If a pipe is kept clean and occasionally rested, then if it is any use at all it ought to offer friendly service for years. Bear in mind, though, that while bowls should be cleaned out not all the carbon inside should be removed, because it keeps the pipe cool.

Tobacco next. I have no statistics but I fancy that twenty-nine out of thirty pipemen smoke the same tobacco year in and year out. This puzzles me. Do they want the same dish for dinner every night? I suspect them of having no interest whatever in tobacco itself. Years ago they discovered 'a good smoke' and ever since have been buying a tin or two of it every week. This is not my style at all, and never was. I like different tobaccos for different times and occasions. And I enjoy experimenting. There can hardly be anything fit to be smoked at all that I haven't tried at some time or other. But here—alas—I must give a warning to young pipesmokers who want to settle down with Dad's favourite old

* Actually the very hard root of a species of *Erica Arborea*, grown in the drier Mediterranean regions.

brand. The sad truth is that many of these favourite old brands have fallen off lamentably during the last ten or fifteen years. It is not that my palate now demands too much; too many popular flakes and mixtures are nothing like as good as they used to be: the flavour and guts have gone out of them.

Having announced this mournful news, I will at least offer the young pipesmoker a useful tip. (But possibly the old pipesmoker, if he has never thought seriously about tobacco, might find my advice even more useful.) If you find the popular old brand, the one your dad used to enjoy, lacking character, tang or bite, then you should proceed to give it some extra flavour yourself. This is done by adding—and mixing in thoroughly—small proportions of what are often called 'seasoning tobaccos', of which the most successful, to my taste, are Latakia, Perique, and a strong black Cavendish. They might be described as the onions, curry powders and peppers of the tobacco cuisine. Latakia and Perique are expensive (I have used for some years a fairly cheap and effective Cavendish), but then you need only add small quantities of them, especially Perique, which is strong and pungent—the black pepper in the dish.

Perique comes from Louisiana, and is a natural dark leaf, which has an unusual curing process and is very finely cut. (Anybody who wants to understand the various curing processes, which give tobacco leaves their particular character and flavour, should consult Mr Alfred Dunhill's book, *The Gentle Art of Smoking*.) Cavendish starts its life as a bright Virginian leaf that is steamed and then pressed into cakes. Latakia, the darling of them all because of its wonderful aroma, comes mostly from Asia Minor and Macedonia, with some inferior contributions from Africa nowadays. It owes its special character to the way in which it is slowly cured by the fumes of smouldering oaks. Because its flavour and fragrance are so rich Latakia was popularly supposed to contain too much nicotine, and I well remember, in the 'thirties, the old man who kept the Greek tobacco shop in Jermyn Street (there no longer) denouncing this legend, telling me he had customers who had smoked nothing else but pure Latakia for years. I have tried this myself, but it is too rich, rather like having Christmas pudding at all meals.

I may be wrong, being no expert, but I am under the impression that Virginian tobacco, apparently so bland and guileless compared with those dark Levantine products, actually has the largest nicotine content. Indeed, I remember a Greek telling me, years ago, that when Greece offered to settle a debt to Britain in tobacco, the cigarette manufacturers here refused the offer: they said Greek tobacco, as opposed to Virginian, was not sufficiently 'habit-forming'. This may or may not be true, but what is certain is that British firms base their trade on Virginian tobaccos. If the British suddenly stopped smoking there would be a financial crisis in the American South. Many of these tobaccos, maybe, have never seen Virginia. But what is called 'Old Belt', the aristocrat of Virginian tobaccos, a reddish leaf with plenty of flavour, still arrives from plantations in the neighbourhood of Richmond. 'Middle Belt' and the various 'bright' or 'golden' Virginians are grown and cured in other Southern states or in Africa. They are all good for blending but always seem to me rather boring, even the best of them, when smoked alone. One of these, unpressed and very finely shredded, is 'Shag', almost forgotten now by pipesmokers. I seem to remember it was Sherlock Holmes's choice; it was certainly never mine.

To my mind Virginian tobaccos are discovered at their best after they have been subjected to various processes that involve enormous hydraulic pressures, blending their several juices, and are then, by subsequent processes, turned into *cakes, flakes, Navy Cuts, rolls* and *twists*. I can still see, with my inner eye, the navvies of my youth carefully cutting and rolling between their palms their *Thick Black Twist*—at 3½d. an ounce. It was a bit too powerful for my taste—though in those days I often smoked *Cut Black Cavendish*, also at 3½d. an ounce—but of its sort it was a fine honest tobacco. Possibly I am now too accustomed to rich mixtures, but I cannot escape the impression that all these Virginian tobaccos on the less-expensive popular level have lost much of their character during these last years, and so are much improved by judicious 'seasoning'. But if you can afford them, the best importers and manufacturers, people like Dunhill, McConnell, or Rattray in Scotland, can still offer you fine examples of Virginian turned into *cakes, flakes* and *cuts*.

I do not know what is happening to pipe tobacco in Russia now, because I prefer to stay away while so many writers are being persecuted there. But when I used to visit the Soviet Union I found its pipe tobacco very unsatisfactory indeed. It was excellent tobacco in itself but it had not been properly cured. If what I heard was true, then there is some sharp irony here. There was, I gathered, a little nation—or at least a considerable group of people—in the far south, where the tobacco was grown, who were expert at curing it fit for the pipe. But they were among those unfortunates who were removed from their homes and scattered into exile by the ruthless Stalin. Now Stalin (I am sorry to say) was a pipesmoker, and because he had banished and scattered all these expert tobacco curers, there was no longer any good pipe tobacco in the Soviet Union. Its dictator was reduced to stuffing his pipes with cigarette tobacco, a wretched substitute that could not possibly be smoked slowly. And may I repeat what is almost the *leit-motif* of this piece—that pipes must be smoked slowly and not be allowed to generate much heat? The pipesmoker, above all, must 'keep his cool'.

While so uncertain about so many things, we British can still be sure of one thing—that to the knowledgeable pipemen of the world our island is the Mecca. Though I have bought a few serviceable briars in France, our British pipes are supreme. So is our tobacco. American pipe tobacco, which I have been compelled to buy when travelling in the United States for weeks on end, is almost always too sweet and sticky, as if were meant to be eaten, not smoked. Most of the Dutch tobacco, now making headway in Britain, is artificially scented, belonging to the perfumery department. South African was not bad years ago, though always too dry, but some presented to me by a friend quite recently seemed to me impossible, as if the sour spirit of Apartheid had ruined it. On the other hand, I cannot praise the tobacco we do not import and blend here but actually grow and attempt to cure on the spot: the only sort I ever tried was horrible.

On my desk, as I write this, is a wide range of tobaccos for blending, many of which I bought some weeks ago at Dunhill's. (The rest I already had.) There they are—from the brightest Light Virginia and Turkey leaf to the mysterious black 'seasoners', Latakia, Perique, and the rest. I am already deciding—to fill one of the four pouches I keep going—on a new mixture, on the dark side—omitting Light Virginia, Turkey, Cigar Leaf (never really successful), using a darker Virginia as base, very little Cavendish, only a pinch or two of Perique, but including rather more Latakia. Hurray! But, however this turns out, I am still left with one nagging thought. These fine mixtures, like everybody else's, tend to be rather dry and so a pipeful of them does not last long enough. What is needed is this type of rich mixture that has a broader cut, to make it last. Does anybody remember now the Craven *Double-Broad*, the creation of a vanished age? I don't ask for its return; I fancy it would seem too mild now; but if this informal piece should catch the eye of any tobacco blender—and it will be a shame if it doesn't—might I suggest he should have a shot at a splendid rich broad-cut? I warn him now, however, that even if he succeeds I may start trying to improve his mixture, gilding his gold, painting his lily.

One last point. It may be that the great brains of our time, like Sir Gerald Nabarro, are right when they fanatically oppose all use of tobacco. Possibly we old pipesmokers already look like a rickety, coughing, choking, pathetic gang of red-eyed addicts. Perhaps if we had to start all over again we would never put a match to a pipe. But I must say I have enjoyed my sixty years of ruining myself, and if, as it is, I have been too often restless, impatient, and perhaps arrogant, without a pipe I would have been ten times worse. Moreover, it happens that the wisest men I have known have been pipesmokers. Of course, there are silly pipesmokers. But they might have been even sillier, more unreasonable, bigger nuisances, more fanatical bashers of other men's little weaknesses, if their pipes had not steadied them down. Oddly enough, most of the notable non-smokers I have known, from Bernard Shaw downwards, could resist the fatal weed but could not resist publicity, pulling faces for press cameras while the rest of us—the weak, the fallen—were simply enjoying a quiet smoke.

Musician-Engraver

THE ENGRAVED GLASSES OF SIMON WHISTLER

LAST YEAR THE SATURDAY BOOK published an account of recent work by Laurence Whistler, who is now recognised as the outstanding glass-engraver in the world. To follow it this year we offer the first illustrations of the work of his son. Simon Whistler was born of the marriage celebrated in his father's prose book, *The Initials in the Heart*, and his sequence of poems, *To Celebrate Her Living;* his mother was Jill Furse, the young actress who died in 1944. He is now thirty-one and has two professions; for he also plays the viola in the London Mozart Players and the Georgian Quartet. Glass engraving and chamber music are of equal importance to him, and he set out on both at about the same time. He was eight or thereabouts when he was given his first violin and also began to learn point engraving from his father. In this technique a diamond or hard steel-point is used to mark the surface of the glass with lines, or with minute dots (known as stippling), or with a combination of both.

As one might expect, many of Simon Whistler's themes have been derived from his life in music. One example was a window-pane for Ivor Newton recording that 'Kirsten Flagstad dedicated this room to Music by singing *An Die Musik*'. Then he has begun to undertake architectural subjects.

In recent years he has developed a style of his own, whose salient qualities are extreme precision, coupled (in pictorial work) with sharp outline. For the first quality, consider 'The Lark Ascending', which is reproduced on the opposite page and which illustrates part of Vaughan Williams's music and Meredith's poem on the same theme, engraved on a Swedish glass nine inches high. The glass is intended to revolve slowly on a turntable so that the first bars of the violin part spiral upwards, like the flight of the bird, in a single stave of music, no less than 34 inches long, which had to be kept regular while smoothly opening out.

One of four decanters given to the Inner Temple in 1962 by
the late Lord Monckton of Brenchley. The decanter illustrated
above shows a view of King's Bench Walk.

Another of the decanters given to the Inner Temple by Lord Monckton, illustrating the Temple Church. On the front side is engraved a Pegasus, and on the other side the donor's initials.

Above: a glass plate, fourteen inches in diameter, given to Szymon Goldberg by the Netherlands Chamber Orchestra on its tenth anniversary. The circle of music is the opening of Bach's *Chaconne for Solo Violin*, engraved so as to be continuously playable. The two dates and violin are engraved in reverse on the underside. 1966

Opposite: one of a pair of decanters given to the Artists Rifles Association by Mr Richard Marriott, representing Mars and Minerva. Minerva is surrounded by instruments of the arts and crafts. 1970

WHO DARES WINS

A goblet given by Captain Stephen Roskill, R.N., in 1970 to his wife Elizabeth as a fortieth-wedding present. It shows their former home, Blounce, in Hampshire. The goblet was made to a shape designed by the engraver's father.

A goblet given by the engraver to his grandparents, Sir Ralph and Lady Furse, for their Golden Wedding, with a view of their home, Halsdon, in Devon. The picture is on the far side of the glass. 1964.

THE FEMALE IMAGE

VIEWED FROM SEVERAL ASPECTS

Little Angels

ROGER PINKHAM

THE VICTORIANS were very unself-conscious and at times very silly. They would have quailed before the knowledge of their psychology that *we* have gained by hindsight—by way of Freud and others—and yet their openness, their naturalness, can be disarming and endearing, if not taken too seriously. A certain misting of the eyes, then, is necessary if we are to look sympathetically over the shoulders of Time at one of their psychological hang-ups—the near-deification of little girls— *near*-deification only, since how could they have become real goddesses in that deeply religious age? The next thing to be was an angel—without wings, of course.

However excruciatingly she might strum the piano, or totter leadenly in her new ballet shoes, little Victoria, in her father's eyes, was no less than an angel. At prayers, in the soft glow of the lamp that seemed to add a nimbus to his darling's shining head, the Victorian paterfamilias must have felt at one not only with his Maker but also with some of the great spirits and myth makers of the age—Charles Dickens, Ruskin, Lewis Carroll, Millais, and a host of eminent painters. All of them had warranted his belief in the myth that little girls were angelic.

To visit the Royal Academy was to find abundant evidence of its hold. Papa would stroll from room to room, admiring here, meditating there, wincing perhaps, occasionally, from an unexpected tug at his soul. These paintings, conceived in light neither natural, nor downright theatrical, and yet too sunny by half for England, seemed specially concerned with textures, like the windows of a draper's or a shoe-shop: the palpability of velvet, the crispness of bows, the glitter of little boots; the spaniel silkiness of hair, the pinkness of skin.

The little angel was depicted not only in her Sunday best. Sometimes, like Ruth,

> . . . She stood among the stooks
> Praising God with sweetest looks.

Sometimes she was carrying a pitcher to a well, or standing, pathetically in rags, but with nobility in her eyes, at some poor cottager's door. Sometimes she was improving the shining hour by handing a gift to a wounded soldier, or picking flowers as 'The Young Botanist'. Sometimes, especially in greeting cards produced towards the end of the century, she was wearing no clothes at all, but was bathing in some idyllic pond or resting on the edge of some decently classical bath. In whatever setting, she was sweet, innocent, idealised—a little angel.

Mr Dickens, more than most, had been responsible for creating the myth; for, however angelic the painters made the girls appear, they could not give them souls. Dickens remedied *that*: dissatisfied with mere goodness he offered a market in the claims of Little Dorrit, or Little Nell, or Florence Dombey. Only mundane persons, surely, could choose other than Little Nell—'dear, gentle, patient, noble Nell!' Even so, the claims of the others do not lag behind. They are superstars of goodness; dutiful, shy, loyal, self-effacing, modest, hypersensitive—possessing every unnatural trait in the canon. And yet they represented their age. In doing so they added to something already there. Dickens sensed his public's interest, and he was intelligent enough to realise that Men of Sentiment had been sentimentalising children since the mid-eighteenth century, especially in Reynolds's and Northcote's paintings.

If it be impossible to imagine Little Nell storming an international beauty contest it is no easier to understand her lack of wanting anything for herself. And yet she had vitality—Carlyle wept at her death, even if Wilde laughed—and was vibrant enough for most to serve as an ideal. In the end she was spiritualised for ever in the photograph on the mantelpiece of prepubescent Lottie, or Victoria, or Kate.

How much of the myth Dickens himself believed is unknowable. It is likely that he responded to it emotionally and yet had reservations about it in real life. There was no reason why the artist and the man should have held similar views—his own relations with women were not plain-sailing, and his domestic life had its conflicts. He could hardly have been unaware of the complexities of reality.

Complexities of life were likely to touch even the growing angel at unexpected times; then her wings might grow percept- ibly smaller and glow less effulgently: for instance, when guilt prompted her to disclose the apple-stealing escapade she had been involved in with her brother, or to mention the seemingly unnecessary and uneventful visits with Jenny (nursemaid) to the gates of, say, Wellington Barracks. Nevertheless these were only slips—in effect, escapades—and, in spite of such trans- gressions, and image-wobble, Papa FORGAVE. He had no intention of using the rod and spoiling the child.

Somebody less complicated, the Rev. Francis Kilvert, also believed firmly that little girls were angels, but he also considered that they should not escape the stick. How Kilvert rates as a man of God is hardly known to us, from his Diary. He certainly works hard, if that is evidence—but what is much more visible is his capacity for endless tumbling in love with small shy girls. He is fascinated by their fidelity, their eyes, their hair, their skins, their innocently exposed limbs—even their bottoms. He is enchanted by the fragility of the female sex of tender years, and extraordinarily unaware how sex-starved he himself is. A delightful numbskull, living with all his senses except the mind, we see him annually surveying the Royal Academy, and on one occasion avoiding the larger, more important paintings, to hover entranced before one whose subject excites him keenly: a study of a girl wrongly punished and taking mild objection to it. It is not, then, too great a surprise to learn that Kilvert's outlook on punishment is that of the Old rather than that of the New Testament, and that on occasion he himself is willing to offer an active arm. He speaks here of Fanny Price:

I sat down by the bed and took her hot little hand. She seemed very feverish but was quite sensible and appeared to be much softened and humble. If so the severe chastizement she has undergone may have had a happy effect and have broken her self-will and cured her of her faults. Her parents very wisely have not spared her nor the rod. She has during the last few weeks been repeatedly stripped and has had her bottom flogged naked with great severity. . . . I asked her mother if it would shame the girl and have a good effect if I were to whip her myself or if she were to flog her in my presence.

One cannot believe, however, that most of the little angels were caught up in these moral torments of Fanny Price. They had other things to think of. Progress had improved on the eighteenth century in leisure facilities: games, dolls, doll's-houses, peep-shows, to name only some indoor amusements, proffered delightful starting-points for invention. From Dolly—in china or wax—it was but a short step across the playroom to a dwelling in miniature, with a front opening to reveal a tiny cramped replica of a London interior. If it was drawing-room or parlour then Morris curtains and Morris wallpapers

Florence Dombey, by William Maw Egley (1826–1916) (Victoria & Albert Museum)

Four aspects of the 'little girl' as seen through Victorian eyes. The Bad Little Girl above, painted by a lesser Victorian artist, is a revealing contrast to the angelic creature clutching the Good Book in the Parian ware figure. Below are two designs for greetings cards, the nude being drawn by William Stephen Coleman (1829–1904) for a Christmas card.

Wishing you a merry Christmas.

Lewis Carroll's photographic preoccupation with little girls has been the subject of cynical comment, but there can be no question of the imaginative skill with which he posed his young sitters and idealised their odd combination of innocence and elegance. The photograph above is one of Aileen Wilson-Todd, taken at Croft Rectory in Yorkshire in 1865.

'The Young Botanist': watercolour drawing by
Edward John Gregory, R.A., 1895 (Private Collection)

lined the reception rooms, with a few spiky bulrushes in a corner pot. But nothing so smart was to be found below stairs, or in the attics. These were the cell-like regions of the serfs who heaved endless quantities of steaming hot water in copper pails up and down stairs, and any amount of coal, in tiny scuttles.

Laved, before the fire, with Pears soap bubbling around her ears as she was deferentially sponged, London's young angel grew up confident that the world adored her; and, she, in turn, cared for the doll's-house, cleaning it, and arranging her dolls, for comfort. Dolly was put to bed beneath a checked counterpane; even Teddy was allowed a place, now and again, in spite of his being a more oafish animal. When the doll's-house palled, there might be Ludo, draughts, or Happy Families, with butchers and bakers grinning facetiously, as though happy to while away the time for her.

When the weather was clement there could be a trip to the Park, trips to the Zoo, or, even better, a trip out from the sun-baked city, to the country. But although an excursion was exciting, since it often disclosed the strange forms of unfamiliar creatures, or magnificent prospects of coast and sea, these events were nothing compared with the pleasures of party-going. Here, our heroine's aim was to be as celestial as was possible: perhaps, if not at one with the angels, then at least on a level with the fairies. Although fairies had an elusive quality, never quite availing of themselves in earthly life, and envied for this anarchical freely-ranging existence, they could at least—if never caught and tamed—be copied. Then the model was likely to be the Fairy Queen in panto, a limelit ambassador in trembling sequins, with magical powers.

Denied a career on the boards because of age, morality and good taste, our heroine could properly copy this image for a special occasion—an oasis in a schoolroom grind of Latin and French irregular verbs. She went scrubbed (and admonished to be only on her best behaviour), accompanied by a stately and possibly apprehensive paterfamilias. He would watch her vanish into the mêlée of her hostess's drawing-room, cocooned in yards of tulle, or silk or humble velveteen livened by ribbons and bows. How vexing if one were late for one of these functions!

Worse still, to be the youngest or the eldest, though there was compensation in the jellies, biscuits and ices. And, perhaps there might be a Boy to bait—a young barnacle of the male sex lodged uneasily at the table-corner, uncertain whether to flee, or to continue, mute. Ultimately, in the best traditions of stumbling and incoherence, this barnacle might introduce himself, and even propose a dance.

When the years of light-hearted party-going were over there might come a period that was haunted by Doubts. No doubts on the part of Little Miss, who was moving quite naturally into puberty; but doubts—and curiosities—in the hearts of her elders. Amongst parents and 'decent people' these doubts could be a matter of genuine concern. At what age *did* sexual capacity begin? But others were not so finicky, as the child prostitutes of Birmingham and the Haymarket could testify.

Fortunately most little angels were blissfully unaware of such blots on Victorian morality, but many of them must have encountered a certain baffling and equivocal reaction on the part of their adult admirers and devotees. In some cases there were undoubtedly attempts to invest the angels with sexual attributes before their wings were dry. That confusion has probably been cleared up by modern thinking, but in an age when chastity and 'soul' were almost synonymous, it is un-surprising that they became mixed. Kilvert (perhaps without noticing) even adds pagan comparisons in the following ecstatic passage in his diary:

> As I walked from Shanklin to Sandown along the cliff edge I stopped to watch some children bathing from the beach directly below. One beautiful girl stood entirely naked on the sand, and there as she half sat, half reclined sideways, leaning upon her elbow with her knees bent and her legs and feet partly drawn back and up, she was a model for a sculptor, there was the supple slender waist, the gentle dawn and tender swell of the bosom and the budding breasts, the graceful rounding of the delicately beautiful limbs and above all the soft and exquisite curves of the rosy dimpled bottom and broad white thigh. Her dark hair fell in thick masses on her white shoulders as she threw her head back and looked out to sea. She seemed a Venus Anadyomene fresh risen from the waves.

If Kilvert is too earthbound to be fully persuaded of the reality of the myth here, and writes for effect (his use of colours being a little too artful), one who *was* galvanised entirely by little angels was Lewis Carroll. Carroll is now, of course, as famous as a photographer as he is as the writer of the Alice books. In many photographs of little girls he sought determinedly to capture their gossamer essence, their charm and sophistication. In spite of their being angels, Carroll's sitters have an unpleasant quality, which comes over distinctly through the highly textured and grainy prints: his sitters have a sulky and rather cross prettiness; they seem about to explode into a tantrum at any moment. Carroll sought out pretty children with the calculation of the persistent lepidopterist. He would even photograph a *boy* if it meant there was a chance to record his prettier sister!

Unlike Kilvert, who accepted little angels wholeheartedly, without critical analysis, Carroll contributed to the legend. He built on accepted lore and gave us Alice, thereby widening and enriching the myth. Behind the courtesy and the tolerance of Alice is a lightning-quick mind and deviousness. She is a 'no nonsense' child, quite liable to kick you in the shins or slam the gate on your hand if it suits her. This edgy quality in Alice is obviously Carroll's, and is characteristic of his restlessness and his eternal quest to create the perfect mythical setting around his little sitters. At one moment they are in costume; the next they are acting out a phantasy, or they appear naked. Carroll had tried photographing boys nude, but had recoiled; they looked simply undressed. The less-skinny female he found ideal, with a loveliness that was perfect. Yet he was not without qualms on the subject:

If I had the loveliest child in the world and found she had a modest shrinking (however slight and however easily overcome) from being taken nude, I should feel it was a solemn duty owed to God to drop the request *altogether*.

In this passage Carroll reveals some interesting personal aspects of himself. The tragi-comic sentiment fits well with his own appearance: to look at, in face, he was a cross between Buster Keaton and Oscar Wilde—sad, ashen and unlaughing. The passage shows too his artistic discretion, and perhaps explains why he cooled so markedly towards his sitters when they grew out of childhood; by then they had lost the sensitivity and plasticity he required to serve his phantasy.

If Ruskin had been creative, and not only an interpreter of art, it is unlikely that he would have been swept off his feet by Rose La Touche, as he was. But in his enthusiasms he never adopted half-measures: Pre-Raphaelitism, Turner, Switzerland, owe him much for the supporting power and interpretive energy he put into them. The meeting with Rose occasioned in Ruskin one of those dry hysterical passions that cannot come to good. It was the biggest shipwreck of his amatory life. He had always evaded by one means or another a complete sexual entanglement. The connexion with a little angel may have struck him as an ideal solution. In *Praeterita* he describes their first meeting:

> So presently the drawing-room door opened, and Rosie came in, quietly taking stock of me with her blue eyes as she walked across the room; gave me her hand, as a good dog gives its paw, and then stood a little back. Nine years old, on 3rd January, 1858, thus rising now towards ten; neither tall nor short for her age; a little stiff in her way of standing. The eyes rather deep blue at that time, and fuller and softer than afterwards. Lips perfectly lovely in profile;– a little too wide, and hard in edge, seen in front; the rest of the features what a fair well-bred Irish girl's usually are; the hair, perhaps, more graceful in short curl round the forehead, and softer than one sees often, in the close-bound tresses above the neck.

What a pity that he did not stop to analyse the implications of the phenomenon, as he had analysed the worlds of Art and Nature. But he did not. The surface was a lovely dream, sufficient in itself; and Ruskin sank into it without noticing that a man of forty and a child of ten must have an unequal relationship at the best of times. At the time it was not, it seems, considered exceptional. So he plunged into the whirlpool of infantilism. But he was neither a deprived sensualist like Kilvert, nor a creative artist like Carroll, but a man needing the challenge of a crusade to measure himself by. But in this case his crusade was founded on nothing more concrete than one of the looser sentiments of the age, and he saw in Rose mainly what he needed to, to formulate a vision. Rose is no Héloïse. She writes:

Drawing of a Girl by Sir John Everett Millais, P.R.A. (Collection, Jeremy Maas, Esq.)

57. DEAREST ST CRUMPET—I am so sorry—I *couldnt* write before, there wasnt one bit of time—I am so sorry you were disappointed—I only got yr letter yesterday (Sunday) & we only got to Nice late on Saturday afternoon—So I have got up so early this morning to try & get a clear hour before breakfast to write to you, which you see I'm doing—So you thought of us, dear St Crumpet, & we too thought so much of you—Thank you very much for the Diary letter; it was so nice of you to write so long a one—I have so much to tell you too Arichigosaurus so I will begin from Dover, & tell what befel us up to Nice—Emily asks me to say that she did a picture of Dover Castle in a fog—I think it was to please you—Well we had a roughish passage. . . .

Yes. In the end she eluded him, as angels will, should they be believed in too idealistically, in a materialistic world.

Victorian Nudes

BY JEREMY MAAS

THERE ARE STILL those to whom a discussion about nudism in Victorian times would suggest a contradiction in terms, as would, say, a consideration of monastic life in the Regency period. Such an attitude is entirely understandable though equally erroneous. Our present-day concept of the Victorians is, above all else, still coloured by notions of piety, prudery, moral rectitude and so on. Nor is this attitude limited to patterns of social behaviour: it also governs our response to their literature and art. When it comes, however, to analysis of what the Victorians *dared* not reveal, literature is a more fashionable and rewarding target. Endless is the speculation as to how Dickens, Thackeray and Hardy might have phrased certain passages in the apparently more permissive climate that we are now said to enjoy.

To most students of the period there comes a time, usually quite early on, when they realise that in many ways the Victorians behaved little differently from ourselves; it is just that in what they did and what they said and what they allowed themselves to see they drew the line quite differently from us. It is a question of emphasis. In matters of outward appearance there was abundant display, sometimes opulent, often vulgar, but with anything to do with what one might call inward appearance—nudity for instance—there was plenty of reticence. It was here, in the dark corridors of the Victorian consciousness, that prim-lipped prudery stalked. It was a prudery that was wholly inconsistent: women may have fainted if they thought they had exposed an ankle, and statues in stately homes were often draped on festive occasions, but how does one explain the young George du Maurier's surprising complaints that women at dinner parties he attended in the 'sixties wore such low *décolletages* that they were in danger of sudden part-frontal nudity; or how does one explain how a courtesan like Skittles could in a seemingly prudish age, flaunt her very obvious charms in Rotten Row among the fashionable set? To say that it was because of her excellent horsemanship is clearly not enough.

How then does one adequately explain the continued existence of nude painting in Victoria's reign, and its final triumph, albeit quantitively, at the close of her reign? The answer, if threefold, is very simple: it was the enormous prestige of art in general and High Art in particular, and most particularly of all the prestige of classical art as a civilising influence in an expanding middle-class society. Neo-classicism was a force in art and had been succesively upheld by Flaxman, Canova, Thorwaldsen, John Gibson and others. Moreover, to the academic mind its attractions were rarely resistible. Never far from the scene was the genuine public enthusiasm for classical antiquity engendered by such great symbols of classicism as the Elgin marbles; the tragi-comic Haydon was for ever bombastically proclaiming the supremacy of the ancient Greeks; whenever, in cultured circles, nude painting was discussed, Praxiteles's name was sooner or later sure to be invoked. And, of course, it was the beauty of the naked form which formed the ultimate in the classical ideal.

Nude painting was therefore blessed, if not divinely, at least with the seal of classical authority, and thus provided an excuse for gazing at the naked female form without feelings of guilt. It was still a slender and vulnerable thing, easily the victim to violent attacks ... the gentle and retiring William Etty, who was reduced to pleading for his voluptuous pictures that 'no immoral sentiment is *intended*', was repeatedly savaged by the attacks of prudish and prurient critics. On one such occasion, in 1839, be bowed momentarily and reinforced the draperies in his 'Pluto carrying off Proserpine'. Happily his contempt for the 'Noodles', as he called his critics, triumphed on the last day of varnishing. 'Took off the thick paint', he wrote 'and restored the transparent.' Again and again Etty was assailed by ferocious attacks in the Press. *The Spectator*, for instance, considered 'The Sirens and Ulysses' 'a disgusting combination of voluptuousness and loathsome putridity'. It was a most fortunate thing indeed that the attacks on Etty and other painters were for the most part confined to London where the most important exhibitions were

William Mulready, R.A.: 'The Bathers', 1849 (National Gallery of Ireland)

William Etty's 'Seated Bacchante' (Private Collection) is an almost aggressively female
nude, the kind that shocked many a visitor to the Royal Academy exhibitions of the
period. It would be fruitless to speculate as to her identity: Etty found his models in
the Life School, members of the foreign colony in Soho, shop assistants glad of pin
money, and occasional paragons, which the Pre-Raphaelites would call 'stunners' and
guard jealously against the predatory instincts of their brethren.

Aquatic settings provided William Frost with fitting opportunities for the display of naked naiads. 'Sabrina' above (M. Newman, Ltd.), which was exhibited at the Royal Academy in 1845, is an illustration to Milton's *Comus* in which the spirit describes Sabrina having fled from her stepdame Guendolen, being borne to the hall of Nereus in the depths of the stream.

Below, an illustration to *A Midsummer Night's Dream*, painted in about 1867 by a little-known artist, who is known to have done at least one other picture illustrating this play.

'The Cave of the Storm Nymphs', by Sir Edward J. Poynter, BT., P.R.A. (Collection, B. A. Skinner, Esq.) is one of those stunning creations which contended for the title 'Picture of the Year'. It was exhibited at the Royal Academy in 1903, a year particularly rich in enormous nude extravaganzas.

held. In his native Yorkshire he was revered, and his mercantile patrons such as Joseph Gillott demonstrated by their patronage that they were quite unmoved by such hostility as there might be in the metropolis. There is a story that Gillott, when walking down Gray's Inn Road early one morning saw a girl run out of a house hurriedly, *décolletée* and beautiful. She was rushed off to Etty who painted her magnificent figure into one of his pictures for Gillott. Sadly the model ran away and was never seen again.

William Frost, a younger contemporary of Etty, painted numerous groups of naked naiads and dryads in sylvan settings often quite as realistically as Etty, but seems to have provoked the critics less. Indeed after Etty's death and civic funeral in his native York in 1849 Frost was the most consistent purveyor of nudity on the walls of the Royal Academy for the next twenty years.

There were several art schools in London where painting from the undraped live figure was taught in the middle years of the nineteenth century, notably Sass's and Heatherley's schools, and the Langham Sketching Club in Clipstone Street. It was here that the young Pre-Raphaelite follower, George Boyce, painted the female nude in 1851 and was on several occasions smitten by the beauty of the models. And then, of course, there was the Life School at the Royal Academy, where Etty used to sit among the students, almost till the end of his life, much to the embarrassment of some of his dignified contemporaries.

The periodicals of the age abound in attacks and counter-attacks on nude painting. The *Art Journal* of the year of the Great Exhibition attacked the writer of a pamphlet for 'taking it for granted that *every one considers an undraped statue to be indelicate*; he does not seem to think that this can be questioned'. The reviewer cites the example of female artists who were condemned 'to dwell in mediocrity for ever, because they almost fear to be let it be known that they draw from plaster casts, much less than living models'. In 1860 it looked dangerously as though govern-ment subsidies to art schools might be withdrawn where it was discovered that students were painting from the living female model. The motion was put forward in the House of

Commons by a morally indignant peer called Haddo. Fortunately
the motion was defeated by a large majority. The Pecksniffian
Lord Haddo had discovered that no less than four out of twelve
schools had dared to adopt the practice of nude female models.

Nude painting, if it did nothing else, at least afforded the
Victorians a useful opportunity of reminding themselves of
what women actually looked like 'in the altogether'. Perhaps
the difficulties in the way of getting women to pose in the nude
might account for the weakness of so much nude painting of
the period. Acquiring even an elementary knowledge of anatomy
was difficult enough. The sculptor John Gibson in his student
days was reduced to body-snatching by the light of a lantern:
coffin after coffin had to be forced open until a suitable corpse
was selected for dissection. All the while the attacks on nude
painting persisted. These included some mindless nonsense by
a writer in the *Art Journal* of 1874, who even extended his strictures
to men, 'with only a narrow strip of covering for their loins'
sporting in the Mediterranean surf. The nadir was reached when
an early precursor of Women's Lib, signing herself 'A British
Matron', wrote a letter to *The Times* attacking nude painting.
The cause was taken up by J. C. Horsley, R.A., who read a paper
to the Church Congress of 1885. 'Clothes Horsley', as he was
nicknamed, makes no mention of this in his memoirs, nor of
Whistler's witticism: 'Horsley soi qui mal y pense'.

The predicament of female artists was perhaps the most
invidious. A state had been reached whereby women had to be
protected from seeing that which they themselves already
possessed, namely, a female body. The artist Louise Jopling wrote
of the 'sixties: 'A female student was not allowed to study from
what is euphoniously [*sic*] called "the altogether" ', sanely adding
that 'it is no shock to a girl student to study from life'. It is small
wonder that Lady Elizabeth Butler devoted her life to painting
elaborate and highly successful battle pictures. Her long dreary
excursions on alternate days, during her student period, to
study from the 'undraped' female model in Bolsover Street
gave her the opportunity of posting herself near the omnibus
door 'to study the horses in motion in the crowded streets'.

A great stir was caused in 1860 when a young woman called

Laura Herford, who was Helen Allingham's aunt, slipped into the Antique School at the Royal Academy. She had initially escaped detection because she had put her initials only on the drawings she submitted. 'Brave pioneer!' Louise Jopling remarked. One wonders what might have happened had she penetrated as far as the life class. One of the few women who succeeded in getting large nude subjects of a frankly voluptuous nature on to the Royal Academy walls year after year was Henrietta Rae (Mrs Ernest Normand). She had studied from the undraped model at a class for women run on co-operative principles in Fitzroy Square. Inevitably she was assailed from every quarter. While she was exhibiting a diaphanous Ariadne at the Royal Academy, shortly after having given birth to a son, a self-appointed guardian of public morals wrote imploring her 'to pause upon the brink' and not pervert her artistic gifts by painting such works. She showed the letter to her doctor who advised her to reply to the charge of lack of impropriety in representing the human form by mentioning the recent birth of a son 'who came into the world entirely naked'. This son, or perhaps his brother, later mutilated one of his mother's pictures while indulging in gymnastic exercises. Ironically, Henrietta Rae was berated by a critic in the Art Journal for clothing her Ariadne too bounteously. Using classicism as her authority and the example of Albert Moore and others, she was able to paint and exhibit further nude extravaganzas, in which the sexes are mixed. 'Eurydice sinking back into Hades', which won prizes at international exhibitions, has an Orpheus forlornly regretting his lethal backward glance, while in 'Zephyrus wooing Flora' of 1888, the almost completely nude hero is, if not actually touching the nude heroine, no further than a millimetre away.

Before this time there had been many precedents involving most of the permutations of nudity. As early as 1865 Albert Moore had exhibited 'The Marble Seat' at the Royal Academy. The subject of the picture makes Manet's 'Déjeuner sur l'herbe', which had closed down the exhibition at the Salon des Refusés two years previously, look like a Vicar's outing. In Moore's picture a nude boy with genitals fully and precisely revealed is pouring wine into a cup; seated on a marble seat are three girls in transparent white draperies. At least two of the girls are looking in the general direction of the boy, and the girl nearest the boy, as a gesture of deference to public morality, is pointedly staring towards the onlooker.

By the 1890's victory could finally be claimed by the nude painters. *Fin-de-Siècle* decadence cleared the way. Painting and sculpture ran riot in its nakedness. Exhibitions abounded with pictures of flat-breasted maidens wearing steel amulets and uncouth military helmets and brandishing spears and swords, and slender boys holding aloft dripping gorgons' heads; hairy warriors returning from wars to be greeted by pullulating swarms of naked slave-girls. In 1896 was published a book, which would now be described as high camp, called *The Nude in Art*, containing forty-five large illustrations of paintings by artists of all nations. To modern eyes growing accustomed to or satiated by the girlie magazines the pictures are hilarious, but to our forefathers the chance to see 'The Disarranged Toilet' by Le Quesne, 'Girl or Vase?' by Siemiradzki, or even 'A visit to Aesculapius' by Poynter, was the most that late Victorian sophisticates could hope for.

Alfred Stevens, a native of Blandford in Dorset, was one of the most gifted draughtsmen of the nineteenth century. He was also a notable sculptor and a portrait painter of rare distinction. This drawing (now in the Tate Gallery) was one of a series discovered early in this century in the lumber of Dorchester House, Park Lane. It is a study for an intended ceiling painting in the dining-room which was never executed, although the furnishings and fittings of the room were completed by Stevens in 1865.

On the left is 'The Three Graces', by Sir Edward Burne-Jones (City Art Gallery, Carlisle), a large pastel drawing done in about 1873. Burne-Jones's essays in nude painting gave him considerable trouble. Six years after having been elected as a member of the Old Water-Colour Society, his fellow members, accustomed to the flaccid historical compositions of Cattermole and others, objected to one of his nude drawings. Burne-Jones refused to alter the offending part with removable chalk, removed the picture from their walls and himself from the Society.

On the right is 'Flora' (Collection, Sebastian de Ferranti, Esq.), by Roddam Spencer Stanhope, who was, to quote his biographer Mrs Stirling, a man of 'joyous temperament, full of irresponsible humour and of a very quaint wit'. He was a protégé of G. F. Watts, although this picture shows to a marked extent his affinity with the pre-Raphaelites, some of whom he met at Little Holland House.

George Frederick Watts, o.m., r.a.: 'Life's Illusions', 1849 (Tate Gallery)

Sir Edward J. Poynter, BT., P.R.A.: 'Andromeda', 1869 (Maas Gallery, London)

On the left: 'Blowing Bubbles', by Arthur Hill (The Fine Art Society) This charming exercise in playful sensuality owes its origin less to any English influence than to the French tradition of boudoir pictures, from the saucy rendering of girls' buttocks by Boucher to the *almost* humorous nude fantasies of Bouguereau, Laurens, Rebouet and other pillars of the Salon tradition. This kind of picture looked equally at home in elegant drawing-rooms furnished in the *Louis Quinze* style and in the plusher establishments of the *demi-monde*.

On the right: 'A Favourite Custom' by Sir Lawrence Alma-Tadema, O.M. R.A., 1909 (Tate Gallery). Although painted some years after Queen Victoria's death, and three years before his own, this picture is ample evidence that Alma-Tadema was far too old a dog to learn new tricks. In virtuosity of handling and choice of subject, the painting shows little advance on similar work of the 1870's But Alma-Tadema was a popular painter and highly esteemed as a person, and was therefore more able than most to withstand even the cruellest whims of fashionable taste. This is further underlined by the fact of its purchase under the terms of the Chantrey bequest, an act which appears now to have been more a gesture of deference to an established reputation than an attempt to recognise new talent.

'The Fair Archers' by George Elger Hicks (Maas Gallery, London)

Bayly Ballads

BY THOMAS HAYNES BAYLY

THE ARCHERY MEETING is fixed for the third;
The fuss that it causes is truly absurd;
I've bought summer bonnets for Rosa and Bess,
And now I must buy each an archery dress!
Without a green suit they would blush to be seen,
And poor little Rosa looks horrid in green!

Poor fat little Rosa! she's shooting all day!
She sends forth an arrow expertly they say;
But 'tis terrible when with exertion she warms,
And she seems to be getting such muscular arms;
And if she should hit, 'twere as well if she missed,
Prize bracelets could never be clasped on her wrist!

Dear Bess with her elegant figure and face,
Looks quite a Diana, the queen of the place;
But as for the shooting—she never takes aim;
She talks so, and laughs so! the beaux are to blame;
She dotes on flirtation—but oh! by-the-bye,
'Twas awkward her shooting out Mrs Flint's eye.

They've made my poor husband an archer elect;
He dresses the part with prodigious effect;
A pair of nankeens, with a belt round his waist,
And a quiver of course in which arrows are placed;
And a bow in his hand—oh, he looks of all things
Like a corpulent Cupid bereft of his wings!

They dance on the lawn, and we mothers, alas!
Must sit on camp stools with our feet in the grass;
My Flora and Bessy no partners attract!
The Archery men are all *cross Beaux* in fact!
Among the young Ladies some *hits* there may be,
But still at my elbow two *misses* I see!

Set to music by G. LINLEY

Oh! when they brought me hither, they wonder'd at
    my wild delight,
    But would I were at home again, I cannot dance to-night!
How can they all look so cheerful? The dance seems strangely
    dull to me;
The music sounds so mournful, what can the reason be?
   Oh! when they brought me hither, they wonder'd at my wild delight,
   But I would I were at home again, I cannot dance to-night!

Hark! Hark! at length he's coming. I'm not weary—let me stay!
I hear his laugh distinctly now, 'twill chase the gloom away.
Oh! would that I were near him, he sees me not amid the crowd,
He hears me not—ah! would I dread to breathe his name aloud.
   Oh! when they brought me hither, they wonder'd at my wild delight,
   But would I were at home again, I cannot dance to-night!

He leaves that group of triflers, and with the smile I love to see,
He seems to seek for some one—oh! is it not for me?
No, no! 'tis for that dark-eyed girl, I see her now return his
    glance,
He passes me, he takes her hand, he leads her to the dance!
   Oh! when they brought me hither, they wonder'd at my wild delight,
   But would I were at home again, I cannot dance to-night!

                     Set to Music by the Author

For fifteen springs I have been out, and I am thirty-three!
I never get proposals now, what can the reason be?
   All strangers guess me twenty-one and praise me to the
   skies,
Because I have such pearly teeth and animated eyes.

Would none but strangers saw me now! Alas, it is my lot
To dwell where I have always dwelt, half rooted to the spot!
Children who shared my childish sports have children of their
    own,
And brats I once look'd down upon are men and women grown!

Last week a gallant son of Mars invited me to dance:
We laughed, we talked! I really thought once more I had a
    chance!
At length he said 'My dear Miss Smith, you don't remember
    me!
I'm William Jones, twelve years ago you danced me on your
    knee!'

When fashionably dress'd, some friend exclaims 'Miss Smith I
    know
You must remember sleeves like these, at least ten years ago.'
The sweetest fruit is that which hangs the longest on the tree,
For fifteen springs I have been out, and I am thirty three!

Set to music by G. LINLEY

O H! NO! we never mention her,
    Her name is never heard,
    My lips are now forbid to speak
That once familiar word:
From sport to sport they hurry me
    To banish my regret:
And when they win a smile from me,
    They think that I forget.

They bid me seek in change of scene
    The charms that others see;
But were I in a foreign land,
    They'd find no change in me:
'Tis true that I behold no more
    The valley where we met;
I do not see the hawthorn tree—
    But how can I forget?

For oh! there are so many things
    Recall the past to me;—
The breeze upon the sunny hills,
    The billows of the sea;

The rosy tint that decks the sky
  Before the sun is set;—
Ay, every leaf I look upon
  Forbids me to forget.

They tell me she is happy now,
  The gayest of the gay;
They hint that she forgets me,
  But heed not what they say:
Like me perhaps she struggles with
  Each feeling of regret;
But if she loves as I have loved,
  She never can forget.

Set to music by SIR HENRY BISHOP

U PBRAID me not, I little heed
  The bitter words you speak:
  The worst reproach that you can use
Is on that faded cheek.
And though a threat would fail to rouse
  My feelings or my fears,
This heart is touch'd by your despair,
  And trembles at your tears.

How well do I remember you
  In all your spring of youth,
Believing each fair word and smile
  Arose from simple truth.
Upbraid me not—the false one scorns
  The threaten'd doom he hears;—
This heart is touched by your despair,
  And trembles at your tears.

Set to music by the Author

Engraving from *The Fly*, 1839, the year in which Thomas Haynes Bayly died, at the age of 43

'Princess Caraboo of Javasu', painted by Benjamin Barker at Bath in 1817
(By courtesy of Sabin Galleries, Cork Street, London)

The Strange Case
of Princess Caraboo

BY CHARLES NEILSON GATTEY

O N THURSDAY EVENING, the third of April, 1817, the
overseer of the poor in the parish of Almondsbury in
Gloucestershire called on the nearest magistrate, Mr
Samuel Worrall, to inform him that a strange young female,
unable to speak the King's English, had entered a cottage in the
village and had made signs that she would like to be allowed
to sleep there. She had spoken in a tongue they could not understand; so, as there was a servant working for Mr Worrall who
knew several foreign languages, he had brought the girl along
to see if this man could help—but the fellow was unable to
understand her either.

The new arrival was five feet two inches tall and wore a black
dress with a frilled muslin collar. There was an oriental look
about the way she had arranged a black cotton shawl on her
head and a red and black one round her shoulders. She was
attractive, with dark eyes and hair, faintly red cheeks, a wide
mouth and full lips. All she had with her was a bundle of
clothes, a piece of soap, a few halfpence and a bad sixpence.

As the stranger, who appeared to be in her middle twenties,
was clearly very fatigued, Mrs Worrall arranged for her to spend
the night in a private room in a nearby public house. There,
when given a cup of tea, she first covered her eyes with her hand
and seemed to repeat a prayer, bowing her head at the end.
She refused a second cup, asking in dumb show for the cup to
be washed first, and when she drank the tea she repeated the
same form of prayer very devoutly.

At seven next morning, which happened to be Good Friday,
Mrs Worrall called at the pub and found the young woman
sitting by the fire in the parlour looking very miserable as she
waited for breakfast. Her face brightened at the sight of the
visitor, who had brought her a change of linen. News of the

mysterious stranger had reached the Vicar and he now called, carrying several books on Eastern countries. He thought it possible that she might recognise some of the places depicted in the illustrations. She nodded excitedly when shown plates of China and made signs indicating that she had come in a ship from there to England.

Mrs Worrall decided to take the foreigner back to her house at Knole. When led into the housekeeper's room, where the servants were at breakfast, the young woman noticed some cross buns on the table and after picking one up and staring at it intently she cut off the cross and placed it in her bosom. Later that morning, after returning from church, the magistrate's wife, still somewhat suspicious, summoned the unknown and said, with the object of catching her off her guard: 'My good young woman, I very much fear that you are imposing on me and that you understand and can answer me in my own language. If so, and distress has driven you to this expedient, make a friend of me. I am a female as yourself, and can feel for you, and will give you money and clothes, and will put you on your way without disclosing your conduct to anyone. But it must be on condition that you speak the truth. If you deceive me, I think it right to inform you that Mr Worrall is a magistrate, and has the power of sending you to prison, committing you to hard labour, and passing you as a vagrant to your own parish.'

The other listened as if she did not understand a word, and began speaking in her unintelligible language. Mrs Worrall then wrote down her own name on paper and pointing at herself showed it to the young woman who responded by crying 'Caraboo!' several times as she, too, pointed at herself.

When shown round some of the rooms at Knole she appeared delighted at seeing some pieces of furniture with Eastern figures upon them, and she made signs that they belonged to her own country or that she had been in the country from whence they came. At dinner she declined all animal food and drank only water. She grimaced and shook her head with repugnance when offered meat, beer and cider.

On the following day Mr Worrall took her before the Mayor in the Council House at Bristol. A magistrate was present who knew several foreign languages and had travelled widely, but he declared that both her language and her manners were such as he had never before come across. It was decided that she should be lodged for the time being in the Poor House.

A few days later Mrs Worrall, feeling worried about what was happening, called at the Poor House and discovered the young woman surrounded by admiring gentlemen who all claimed to be experienced travellers. Doubtful as to the propriety of this, Mrs Worrall took Caraboo away to her husband's office in Bristol and left her in charge of the housekeeper for the next ten days.

Daily efforts were made in vain to identify her country of origin. At last a Portuguese from the Malay peninsula was introduced to her, and declared that she was a person of consequence, had been kidnapped from an island in the East Indies, and brought to England against her consent. He alleged that the language she spoke was not a pure dialect, but a mixture of tongues used on the coast of Sumatra.

Impressed to learn that Caraboo had social standing, Mrs Worrall took her back to Knole, where she treated her with due deference. After extensive enquiries she learnt of another gentleman who had travelled widely in the East and invited him to visit her and see what he could make of her guest.

The investigator was fascinated by Caraboo and eventually related to his hostess a most remarkable story, either extracted from the girl herself by signs and gestures, or possibly, in the warmth of his anxiety to discover her history, unconsciously supplied by his own imagination. According to him, Caraboo was a Princess from Javasu, which she said was an island in the East Indies. Her mother was a Malay who had been killed by cannibals called 'Boogoos'. Her father, Jessu Mandu, came from China. He had three other wives and was aged forty-seven, which she explained by tying knots in a piece of string. His people knelt on one knee before her and on both knees before him. One day when walking in the palace garden with three of her ladies she had been seized by pirates who sold her to the captain of a brig. He so ill-treated her that when after eleven weeks they reached Europe and were sailing along the English coast she jumped overboard and swam ashore. Making her way to a cottage with a green door, she was befriended by the woman who owned it, receiving food and dry clothes in exchange for her wet gold-embroidered robes. She had then wandered for six weeks until she reached Almondsbury.

Feeling that Princess Caraboo should now be dressed in a manner befitting her rank, Mrs Worrall gave her a length of calico, out of which the girl proceeded to make a garment very short in the skirt and with uncommonly wide sleeves which almost touched the ground. It had a very broad band round the waist which she embroidered.

During the time Caraboo lived at Knole and Bristol she was never heard to pronounce a word or syllable which resembled English. The housekeeper who slept with her began to pick up a smattering of the outlandish tongue from the vocabulary from which the stranger was careful never to deviate, even employing the same gestures and facial expressions when uttering certain words. The servants once said in her hearing that they would lie awake so as to overhear anything she might say in her sleep. That night and on subsequent ones she pretended to be dreaming and babbled away in her bizarre language to the disappointment of the listeners. When returning sometimes from Bristol in Mrs Worrall's carriage, she would fall into a slumber from fatigue, and even when abruptly roused she never let a word escape her which was not in her own strange tongue.

In the choice of her food Caraboo was also equally consistent. She was very fond of Indian curry, which she frequently prepared herself and made very savoury. She always said her prayers, night and morning, and she fasted every Tuesday, when she would climb on to the roof of the mansion and remain perched perilously there all day. She converted an arbour into a sort of temple where she worshipped her God, Allah Tallah. Before entering this, she would kneel by the pond in Knole Park and wash her face in its water; once she even plunged into it.

Occasionally she would parade round the park, wearing a head-dress of feathers and flowers, armed with a bow and arrows slung from her left shoulder, and with a stick thrust through her belt as if it were a sword. She carried a gong on her back which she sounded from time to time. On some occasions she would use a tambourine instead.

She was an expert fencer. Mr Worrall, who had been a fine swordsman when young, could seldom disarm her. She danced with grace and her manners in company could not be faulted. She became a great favourite with the 'quality'.

A clergyman from Bath, experienced in the wiles of rogues and tricksters, visited Knole to study Princess Caraboo. He decided by means of flattery to discover whether she understood English. He seated himself next to her and fixing her with a look of assumed admiration exclaimed: 'You are the most beautiful creature I ever beheld—you are an angel!' But Caraboo remained impassive, as if she had not understood a word.

Then one day the Princess vanished, wearing the same clothes in which she had arrived and taking nothing else away with her. Mrs Worrall was distraught till she succeeded in tracing the fugitive to Bath, where she discovered her in the drawing-room of a lady of *haut ton*. It was crowded with fashionable visitors, all eager to be introduced to the fascinating foreigner. One was kneeling before her, a second held her hand, another begged a kiss. At the sight of her benefactress Caraboo rushed to her and embraced her most tenderly, then indicated that the escapade had for motive a sudden longing to return home to Javasu.

Whilst in Bath the Princess had her portrait painted by an eminent local painter, Benjamin Barker, and she found a champion in a Dr Wilkinson who wrote articles about her in the *Bath Chronicle* and the *Bristol Journal*. These were reproduced in the national press. But the publicity led to a shattering of the myth. A Mrs Neal of Bristol, curious to see the prodigy, watched for her at the Pump Rooms at Bath and recognised her as Mary Willcocks, a servant girl, who had once lodged with her. Confronted with this former landlady the charming impostor conceded defeat, and confessed all.

The interest aroused in the case led to a detailed investigation into the girl's past. It was found that she had been born at Witheridge in Devon, in 1791, the daughter of a cobbler, and had received no education, being of a wild disposition. From childhood she had always wanted to outshine her companions.

At the age of sixteen she became a nursery maid, and after two years left this situation when refused an increase in her wages from eightpence to a shilling a week. She then decided to try her luck in London. Having no money she begged at houses on the way. Some gave her a little whilst one man threatened to have her arrested as a vagrant and horse-whipped. She was so ill by the time she reached her goal that she collapsed and was taken to St Giles's Hospital, where she remained many months with brain fever.

When Mary recovered, a clergyman found her a place with a Mrs Matthews in Clapham. Here she was well treated and taught to read and write. But after three years she was dismissed for the trivial offence of attending a Jew's wedding.

Mary had often noticed the Magdalen in Blackfriars Road, and had assumed it to be a nunnery. She learnt that women were admitted if they called there on the first Wednesday in a month. This she did. She was asked by the lady in charge questions the meaning of which she did not at the time understand. How long had she gone on in that way? How long had she been on the town? Mary thought the best things to say were that she was sorry for her sins and wanted to lead a virtuous life in future. The lady then told her that as she was so young, if she were truly penitent, they would take her in. Tears prevented Mary from answering. Then her interrogator said gently: 'You poor thing, you are very much affected. We will admit you.'

The weeping girl was given a bath, and donned the Magdalen dress. She remained in this institution for six months and acted as a sort of housemaid. Then one day one of her young companions began describing the details of her own former life. Horrified to discover that the place was a home for fallen women, Mary had an attack of hysterics and when the warden learnt the reason for this she was scolded and turned out for having wormed her way in under false pretences.

Mary Willcocks thought of returning to Devon, but it meant walking over Hounslow Heath. Because of the robberies and murders which took place there, she exchanged her clothes at a pawnbroker's for male attire. Thus disguised she fell in with some highwaymen who engaged her to look after their horses.

But when they tried to teach her to fire a pistol she screamed and they guessed her sex. After she had sworn not to betray them, they gave her a guinea and she went in women's clothing to her home in Witheridge. Her parents found her a place with a tanner in Crediton, but after three months she left because she objected to having to heave the hides out of the carts.

Eventually Mary returned to London, where she was employed by a lady fishmonger in Dark-house Lane, Billingsgate. One day she went to a stationer to fetch some books and here she met and became friendly with an Eastern gentleman, a Mr Baker-stendht, to whom, she subsequently claimed, she was married by a Romish priest. From her husband and his friends she picked up a smattering of Malay and Arabic as well as some knowledge of the Orient and its customs. When staying in Brighton, the new Mrs Bakerstendht found she was pregnant. On learning this her spouse gave her some money and sent her back to London whilst he continued on his way to the Continent. This was the last she ever saw of him. She returned to service, working for a Mrs Clark at the Crab-tree public house in Totten-ham Court Road, till she was taken in labour. Mrs Clark got a coach and took her to the City Road Hospital. She was there three weeks and then left the infant at the Foundling Hospital where it died a month or so later.

The deserted Mrs Bakerstendht once more rejoined her parents. After staying ten days with them, she left in search of another situation. On the road between Exeter and Plymouth she fell in with some gipsies who tried to persuade her to join them but she refused. She started pretending to be a foreigner who had lost her way and by this means obtained free lodging and money from the credulous. She met with such success that she decided to pose as Princess Caraboo.

Mrs Worrall had become very fond of her protégée, and when she had heard the sad story of her life, and had checked up as far as was possible on its accuracy, she felt sorry for the young woman who now said that she wanted to emigrate to America. So the kind-hearted Mrs Worrall bought a passage for her on the *Robert and Ann*, which was about to sail from Bristol to Phila-delphia, and also provided her with clothes and money to support her till she could find employment in the New World. Three young Bristol ladies who were going out to teach in a Moravian settlement were prevailed upon to protect the lone emigrant on the voyage.

Before the departure of the pseudo-princess the public clamoured to gain a sight of her. It was reported that 'the Earl of C——k has come from Bath for the sole purpose of conversing with her, and the Marquis of S——y has written to request the same indulgence.' She was in fact visited by persons from all walks of life—linguists, painters, physiognomists, craniologists wanting to feel her bumps and gipsies eager to tell her fortune. Some pitied her, some condemned her, and others championed her. She herself showed no signs of being sorry for what she had done but appeared highly gratified by the number of persons she had gulled.

Later that same year the following appeared in Felix Farley's *Bristol Journal* for 13 September 1817:

The editor of this Journal is most truly happy in being enabled, through the medium of an Amanuensis employed in the State Paper Office, to communicate the following original intelligence relative to no less a person than that celebrated Female Impostor Caraboo! . . .

A Letter from Sir Hudson Lowe, lately received from St. Helena, forms at present the leading topic of conversation in the higher circles. It states that on the day preceding the date of the last dispatches . . . a boat was seen entering the harbour. Sir Hudson went alone to the beach and to his astonishment saw a female of interesting appearance drop the oars and spring to land. She stated that she had sailed from Bristol in the 'Robert and Ann' . . . that the vessel being driven out of its course by a tempest, when at last the crew perceived land the Captain recognized it to be St. Helena; that she immediately conceived an ardent desire of seeing the man with whose future fortunes she was persuaded that her own were mysteriously connected . . . But finding the Captain resolved to proceed according to his original destination, she watched her opportunity and springing with a large clasp knife into a small boat which was slung at the stern, she cut the ropes, dropped safely into the ocean and rowed away. The wind was too strong from land to allow of the vessel being brought about to thwart her object.

According to the *Bristol Journal* Sir Hudson in his letter went on to describe how Bonaparte was captivated by Caraboo and asked for her to be given an apartment in his house, declaring that she alone was an adequate solace in his captivity. The report ended: 'He has intimated to Sir Hudson his determination to apply to the Pope for a dispensation to dissolve his marriage with Maria Louisa and to sanction his indissoluble union with the enchanting Caraboo.'

Some credulous people in Bristol took all this seriously. The newspaper never referred to this unlikely romance again and as the 'Princess' landed safely in America and lived there for seven years one must assume that it was some kind of a hoax. In 1824 the 'Princess' was once again in London, trying to raise money by exhibiting herself in a back room in Bond Street at an admission charge of one shilling per person, but she attracted very little attention. The next few years she seems to have spent travelling in France and Spain, possibly in search of her vanished husband, Mr Bakerstendht. She must have presumed him dead, for when next one hears of her she had a daughter.

A correspondent to *Notes and Queries* for 20 May 1865, wrote:

I became acquainted with her in Bristol in December, 1849, when, after much reluctance, she gave me her signature as Mary Baker. She then lived under Pyle Hill, Bedminster . . . She avoided as much as possible any conversation with regard to her former career, of which I think she was much ashamed, and nothing annoyed her more than when a neighbour's child ventured to call after her 'Caraboo!'

Mary had died the previous December, aged seventy-two. *The Times* for 13 January 1865 contained the following paragraph:

Such of our readers as are interested in the history of impostors will remember that many years since a person who styled herself the 'Princess Caraboo' created a sensation in the literary and fashionable circles of Bath and other places, which lasted till it was discovered that the whole affair was a romance, cleverly sustained and acted out by a young and prepossessing girl. On being deposed from the honours which had been accorded to her, the 'Princess' accepted the situation, retired into comparatively humble life, and married. There was a kind of grim humour in the occupation which she subsequently followed—that of importer of leeches; but she conducted her operations with much judgment and ability, and carried on her trade with credit to herself and satisfaction to her customers. The quondam 'Princess' died recently at Bristol leaving a daughter, who, like her mother, is said to be possessed of considerable personal attractions.

American Pin-Ups
1870–1900

BY PHILIP KAPLAN

To represent the beauty of one's own time, its very symbol, is a peculiarly aristocratic form of immortality. It is nearest to the fame of the gods.

RICHARD LE GALLIENNE

GLAMOUR PHOTOGRAPHY had its remarkable rise in the carefree 1870's in America, with the expanded use of photography as a news medium. The half-tone printing process had not yet replaced the crude woodcut, and a striking likeness could only be reproduced by photographic means.

The introduction of 'Cabinet' photography in 1866 was an important contribution to glamour photography. Larger than the cheap *carte-de-visite* photo cards the public had been buying for nearly twenty years, the more expensive cabinet photograph was a mounted print which measured $6\frac{1}{2}$ by $4\frac{1}{2}$ inches. While the *carte-de-visite* could be taken in the photographic studio in a few seconds, the new cabinet photograph required a longer exposure, thus qualifying for more serious artistic consideration. With the development of sharper lenses, faster plates and dramatic 'Rembrandt-type' lighting techniques, a large clear photographic image appeared, to delight the public. Although the same instruments of torture—the head-clamp and back-brace—were still in use, photographers' studios were suddenly calling themselves High-class Portrait Palaces and Photographic Art Salons.

The familiar advertising slogan, 'The Camera Does Not Lie', was abruptly discarded in 1869 when James F. Ryder, a leading American photographer, introduced the fine art of retouching. The leading photo gallery 'operators' were quick to pick up the skill. As warts, pimples and crows' feet magically disappeared from their negatives, actresses and leading public figures became even more interested in photographic exposure.

In 1869 the musical revue *British Blondes* burst upon the New York theatrical scene, setting the pattern for burlesque as we know it today. The success of this extravaganza was due to the combined talents and personal charms of four British beauties: Pauline Markham, Lydia Thompson, Ada Harley and Lisa Weber. 'Miss Markham', wrote one critic, 'comes as near a personal realisation of the goddess of loveliness as one can expect.' When cabinet photographs of Miss Markham in tights went on sale at the theatre they were snapped up with enthusiasm. American theatre-goers had been treated to the sight of a well-rounded thigh, and they were eager to take home this daring souvenir of the show. Miss Markham found herself besieged by 'spoons' (the mashers of the day), who now begged for photographs besides the more traditional favours.

Impressed with the potential of this photographic craze, ambitious 'bulb squeezers' sought out the leading glamour figures of the 'seventies. Competition among studios was keen, and top actresses could demand high fees for an afternoon of picture-taking. Photographic exposure was good box office. These young actresses who could project the right mixture of charm and sex-appeal for the camera caught the public's fancy immediately.

Olive Logan, a leading lady of the American stage, tried to explain the photographic craze:

> Why do they buy the photographs? They buy them because they like us, because they don't know us, because they want to see how we look, and for no reason whatever. The photographic market has many fluctuations. Let us be maligned or lauded, scathed or flattered—cabinet photo stock goes up forthwith. Ah, if only we were considerate enough to *die*. What a demand there would be for our photographs then!

'The Simple Seventies', as they were sometimes called, were in fact quite demanding for those who wished to be fashionable, and the latest glamour photographs were examined scrupulously for fashion trends. Dressmakers were kept busy executing new versions of the Grecian Bend, or the popular Swan silhouette, with its bustled back. Both men and women were slaves to fashion. New fads piled one upon another, resulting in overdressing to a ludicrous extreme. Brightly striped materials, and furs and laces of all sorts were bought up eagerly—and worn all at one time. Elaborate coiffures were topped by wide-brimmed hats, outrageously trimmed with flowers, feathers and stuffed birds. The men did their best to keep up with the ladies, sporting top hats and fancy canes, and attired in frock coats, striped trousers and broad knotted ties. Not to be outdone by the latest feminine hair-styles, men blossomed out in flowing beards and heavily waxed mustaches. In such an atmosphere of fashion extravagance, great attention was paid to the costumes of leading actors and actresses and prominent socialites of the day.

One of the most influential glamour figures was the actress Fanny Davenport, whose rich and handsome wardrobe was the envy of all women. Captured by Sarony's lens at the supreme moment of her beauty, Miss Davenport's photographs were eagerly bought up by an adoring public. Her performance as Rosalind in *As You Like It* set the standard for American beauty in the 1870's. One enraptured critic declared: 'She is first a buxom beauty, and then a saucy boy.' For the matinée performances of *Pique*, in which Miss Davenport starred during the 1875–6 Broadway season, a solid silver ticket and a satin programme containing a Sarony portrait of Miss Davenport were given away to every lady in the audience.

The man who pioneered the art of glamour photography was a five-foot wizard named Napoleon Sarony. Born in Quebec in 1821, the son of German parents, Sarony began his career in photography while working with his brother Otto in London. In 1864 he opened his first studio in New York. Within ten years he had moved to larger quarters at 37 Union Square, and the most glamorous women of the day were eager to pose for him.

A genuine eccentric, Sarony was most often dressed in a monkey jacket, with wide trousers tucked into his polished Hessian boots. This outlandish costume was completed by an undyed Astrakhan jacket, fur side out, and a Turkish fez.

Sarony's studio quickly acquired a character as bizarre as its owner. Anyone with a weird or unusual item to sell found his way to 37 Union Square. In a short time the building was crammed with Egyptian mummys, exotic stuffed birds, Russian sleighs,

Chinese temple gods, medieval instruments of torture, and hundreds of strange objects from all parts of the globe. The macabre effect was further enhanced by the malodorous fumes which arose from the photographic laboratory.

The efficiency with which Sarony handled his clients was the envy of his colleagues. Most important to the Sarony photograph was the hint of passion behind the well-coiffed head. To catch that moment of dramatic intensity, Sarony left the actual camerawork to his skilled assistants, while he concentrated on posing his subjects and encouraging them to play to the camera as though to a live audience. One secret in the pose was the high position of the chin, which gave a certain mystery and allure to the face. Lily Langtry, the much-photographed 'Jersey Lily', had this to say about posing:

There are two varieties of photographic expression. Number One: look calm and intellectual. Number Two: look up, look lively, smile a little. I long ago came to the conclusion that there is no headrest for the wicked who come to get photographed. The photographer, taking aim with his chemical-stained finger at the apex, begins moving the former slowly along the regions of nowhere. Ten seconds pass, then a hundred thousand million seconds of agonizing quietude—and your photograph is taken. But then he announces that it must be done all over again! He says I *moved*.

By 1880 Napoleon Sarony had amassed a photographic stock of over forty thousand negatives. While most of the photographs were of the Glamour People (to whom he paid large sums for exclusive rights), his collection also included lecturers, wrestlers and prize-fighters, midgets, religious figures, politicians and famous people linked with the scandals of the day.

Among Sarony's many glamorous subjects was the actress Eileen Karl, who was reported to be 'among the small array of theatrical women who can afford to wear tights and a waist at the same time, without the least want of propriety, without displeasing the most scrupulous artistic eye, and without resorting to padding or improving the figure in any way'. For those who are interested in the 'perfect' feminine measurements of the 1870's, we provide Miss Karl's vital statistics: Height 5 ft 5 in.; weight 160 lb; ankle 6 in.; thigh 35 in.; waist 23 in.; bust 40 in. If

Miss Karl's charms seem generous when compared to our present standards, let us hasten to explain that 'Miss Karl is descended from a French father and an English mother, and seems to combine the voluptuousness of the Gallic race with the sturdiness of the English.'

Sarony's closest competitor was José Maria Mora, born in Cuba in 1849. The son of a wealthy Cuban planter, young Mora was sent to Europe to study art, but instead became interested in photography. In 1869, following the Cuban revolution, Mora joined his family in New York, where he found work as an assistant to Sarony. After observing the master's techniques for a short time, Mora went into photography on his own.

Although still in his twenties, Mora quickly achieved fame for his glamour photographs of famous actresses, and he was among the best known of the first-nighters on the New York theatrical scene. Mora's studio bore a deliberate resemblance to a bare stage; once the shooting began, however, props and backdrops of every description were brought out to dress the stage. Famed for his elaborate photographic effects, Mora's settings included rustic benches, marble columns, gilded fireplaces, papier-maché rocks, and an astonishing collection of over 150 painted back-drops—from polar wastes to tropic isles. Among Mora's most famous photographs were the snow scenes he produced in his studio for 'The Two Orphans' and 'The Snow Flower'. Equally renowned as a Society photographer, Mora was frequently chosen to photograph New York's most elegant social events, including the lavish *bals masqués*.

Mora's style in glamour photography paid off well. Equipped with a large and efficient staff, his gross business had approached 100,000 dollars by 1878. Most of the money was earned by Mora's 'publics'—stock photos of stars who posed for him and were paid on a royalty basis. Maud Branscombe was represented in stock by over three hundred different poses, and over thirty-five thousand of her photos were sold in a short time to her adoring public. Also popular was young Mary Anderson, acclaimed by critics as 'the most beautiful woman on and off stage.' Although Mora's was the largest photo business in the country during the 1870's, there were many other outstanding

American photographers, including Bogardus, Bradley & Rulofson, Howell, Gurney, Kurz and Fredericks.

While the Americans had taken the lead in the business of glamour photography, European photographers were quick to catch up. English photographers had their own ideas of what the public wanted, and they produced elegant photographs of all the members of the Royal and Imperial Families of Europe. Celebrities in the fields of art, science and politics were also photographed for stock photo sales. Leading glamour photographers in England at the time were Herbert Barraud, the Messrs Bassano, W. & D. Downey, Elliot & Fry, the London Stereoscopic Company, Van der Weyde, and many others.

In France the great Nadar (Félix Tournachon) was more involved in the making of history than glamour photography. Nadar's magnificent photographs of his contemporaries are considered works of art today. But the American approach to glamour was found to be so popular in France that Paris studios were using American negatives and crediting the photos, 'Photographie Américaine'.

The family photo album had been the highlight of many a dull evening at home. Now, as sales of glamour photos soared, the modest album underwent an extraordinary face-lift. Photographs of Fanny Davenport and Sarah Bernhardt appeared among the maiden aunts and cousins. Eager collectors splurged on magnificent albums of plush and silk, with ornate silver locks and buckles. Some photo albums had concealed music boxes to add to the pleasures of viewing. The family spent whole evenings arranging their favourite photos in the elaborately-decorated album which now occupied a place of honour on the marble-topped table in the parlour. (A different sort of album, this one with photos of the ladies of the chorus in tights or other indelicate attire, was reserved for those 'connoisseurs' who already appreciated photography as an art form!) With retail prices at $12 for a dozen photos, the family album could be a costly item, but it provided the best in home entertainment at the time.

Lily Langtry provides a humorous insight into the period:

The photographic craze, like every other fashionable rage, has its comic side. After the shopkeepers had exhibited my pictures in the windows alongside royalty and distinguished statesmen, all the pretty women rushed pell-mell to be photographed, that they too, might be placed on view. Some smothered themselves in furs to brave photographic snowstorms. Some sat in swings, some lolled dreamily in hammocks, others carried huge bunches of flowers indigenous to the dusty studio and looking painfully artificial. One lady was actually reproduced gazing at a dead fish! I myself, on one occasion only, gave his head to the photographer who represented me with a dead bird in my hand and an expression of grief on my face—an inspiration of his own which I suppose was designed to touch the heart of the sentimental public.

A latecomer to the New York photographic scene was Benjamin Joseph Falk, who specialised in theatrical photos. From 1884 to 1891 Falk accumulated thousands of stock photographs of the stars. Falk's automatic printing machine, built in 1892, was the first to utilise mass-production techniques to handle the demands of the photo-hungry public. Another Falk speciality was the allegorical photograph which illustrated a well-known fictional or historical scene, or a Biblical tableau. His trick photos of ladies flying through space, swinging from bell-ropes high in church steeples, or cast upon the Rock of Ages, had great sentimental appeal. In general, Falk's touch was light and whimsical, and the public loved his gay approach to the 'nineties.

By 1900 the beautiful cabinet photograph was on the way out, replaced by a garish, highly coloured photographic reproduction. With new and rapid advances in printing techniques, numerous cheap periodicals were springing up to devote entire issues to the glamour personalities of Stage and Society. Pin-up photos were to be seen in every barber shop and saloon. From Klondike mining camp in the far North to freight-train caboose headed south, the entire country was hung with glamour photos.

But 'glamour'—that mystical and elusive quality once so highly prized—had been vulgarised by mass exposure. The 'Simple Seventies', 'Elegant Eighties' and 'Naughty Nineties' had given way to the prosaic twentieth century.

SARONY

On the right is a self-portrait of Napoleon Sarony, the eccentric five-foot photographer who opened his first studio in New York in 1864. Below are two of his characteristic studies of glamorous girls of his time. On the left is the actress Minnie Maddern, subsequently Mrs Fiske, in a hair-style distinctly unusual for its period, and on the right is the famous Adah Isaacs Menken, the American actress and poetess, who was born in New Orleans in 1835, and died in 1868. Married at least four times, once to the boxer Heenan, she made a famous appearance in *Mazeppa* in London in 1864. Among her friends were Gautier, the elder Dumas, Dickens and Swinburne, whose poem 'Dolores' was inspired by her.

223

SARONY

After Sarony's death in 1896 cabinet photos were still being made in his style by a successor. On the left is Marie Doro, one of the earliest movie stars, photographed about the year 1900. The original Sarony took the photographs below. On the left is Lillian Douglas, and on the right is Olga Nethersole, born in 1870, photographed as Carmen in 1896.

Three actresses in costume. On the right is Marie Tempest, photographed by Sarony at 37 Union Square in 1892, at the age of twenty-six, in *The Fencing Master*. Below, on the right, is Eileen Karl, 'who can afford to wear tights and a waist at the same time without resorting to padding or improving the figure in any way'. Her vital statistics were 40–23–35. On the left, below, is Pauline Markham, one of the original *British Blondes* company, as Robinson Crusoe in pantomime.

SARONY

On the right is Fanny Davenport as Rosalind in *As You Like It*, photographed by Sarony—'first a buxom beauty, then a saucy boy'. For many years her photographs were in immense demand. Above is Grace Rawlinson photographed by Howell.

MORA

Cora Pearl, above, photographed by Howell, was one of the notorious courtesans of the 'seventies. Lydia Thompson, on the left, photographed by Mora, was one of the *British Blondes* company, which in 1869 had set the pattern for Broadway burlesque.

MORA

José Maria Mora, son of a wealthy Cuban planter, became an assistant to Sarony in 1869 and then opened his own studio, attracting many famous actresses. On the left is Lilian Russell in *The Snake Charmer*, 1881. Below, on the right, is Maude Branscombe, the musical comedy actress, whom Mora photographed in three hundred poses. On her left is Venie Clancey, actress and singer, photographed about 1877.

228

MORA

Mora had an elaborate studio, rigged up with every sort of scenic effect and a collection of over 150 painted back-drops. Such was the beauty of some of his sitters, however, that he used no props to glamorise them. On the right is his cabinet portrait of Rosa Rand. Below are Jobyna Howland, the original Gibson Girl, photographed about 1900, and, on the right, Evelyn Nesbit, photographed in 1901.

229

Benjamin Joseph Falk, a latecomer to the photographic scene, specialised in theatrical photographs from 1884 to 1891. On the right is Louise Montague, photographed about 1880. Above is Jennie Joyce, photographed in 1891, when Falk had moved his studio from West 24th Street to 949 Broadway.

FALK

Falk's automatic printing machine, built in 1892, was the first to use mass-production methods to produce glamour photographs in quantity. Above is his portrait of Belle Archer, done when his studio was in Broadway, and on the left are Bessie Tyree and Isobel Irving, photographed in *The Amazons* in 1894.

Falk specialised in allegorical photographs—trick photographs which had great sentimental appeal, especially if the 'sitter' was, or appeared to be, flying. Above is Mrs Charles Watson, 1884, enacting the lines from *The Curfew*: 'Out she swung, far out. The city seemed a speck of light below.' On the right is Preciosa Grigolatis as 'The Flying Fairy'.

FALK

Well-known fictional scenes or Biblical tableaux were ingeniously re-created by Falk as a means of projecting the charms of his theatrical clientèle. Above is Ida Muller, as Cupid without any visible means of support, and on the left is Victory Bateman cast up upon the Rock of Ages, a nice combination of glamour and God.

In the wake of Sarony, Mora and Falk came many other photographers of glamour, in and out of New York. On the left is a study of a beautifully tailored lady of 1886, Christie McDonald photographed at Ye Rose Studio in Providence, Rhode Island. Photographs such as this had an immense influence in establishing fashions for the Woman of Elegance.

234

Gilbert & Bacon, of Philadelphia, took this daring and astonishingly 'modern' photograph of Clara Louise Kellogg, who lived to the age of 74 but was presumably in her late twenties when this portrait was made.

Not only actresses were subject to popular exposure. This portrait—photographer unknown—shows the painter and diarist Marie Bashkirtseff, in 1885. The photograph has printed below it the words of François Coppée: *'Je ne l'ai vue qu'une fois, je ne l'ai vue qu'une heure . . . Je ne l'oublierai jamais'*.

235

This striking and famous portrait study of the great and serious actress, Sarah Bernhardt, was taken and reproduced in thousands by Woodburytype.

Ladies on the Scaffold

BY CHARLES GIBBS-SMITH

T HE ILLUSTRATIONS which follow may seem distasteful—
even morbid—to some, but of great fascination to many
others. In a world besotted with violence, with bishops
and prime ministers among the most devoted afficionados of
murder fiction, and millions of ordinary citizens goggling at
monstrous mayhem every evening on their television screens,
the judicial execution of a woman is very seldom shown. Yet
executions are no more, and very often much less, violent than
punch-ups, stabbings, shootings, and all the rest. Premeditated
cold-blooded murder is quite respectable. But not the deliberate
execution of a woman.

The Beheading of Leonora Galigaï in Paris, July 8, 1617

Why should the quick, clean beheading of a queen, for example, be looked upon as something morbid, as opposed to the slow and messy slaughter we are often asked to witness on TV or cinema screens? The truth is surely to be found lying deep in the subconscious layers of men's minds. First, there are often pronounced guilt-feelings associated with what a psychiatrist once called a 'frightful-delightful' sensation. This is only natural when one considers that women are the first objects of infantile hate as well as love, the first sources of food-supply, the first deprivers, the first thwarters of desire, the first spoil-sports, the first punishers, and the first targets of aggression. The more energetic, virile, and individualistic the infant, the more repressive is the behaviour of those who command him; and those who command him until the basic emotions have been stamped into the structure of his soul are, of course, women. Add to this the fact that women are also the first objects of sex and affection in the child from a very early age, and the inevitably forbidden objects where sex is concerned, and one can see that the results add up to a veritable witches' cauldron of seething emotion.

Since all infantile sex and aggression is thwarted at best, and punished at worst, the child grows up learning to associate the mere urge to aggression with the promise of punishment; and as aggressive acts give way under pressure to become aggressive thoughts, physical punishments give way and become feelings of guilt. All guilt is the in-turned transmogrification of what was once externally applied punishment. So, when an aggressive urge arises in the mind, it immediately arouses feelings of guilt, the original reasons for the guilt being lost among the variegated repressions of childhood. According to the infinite varieties of structure in the human mind, guilt plays a greater or lesser part in all our lives; sometimes it is an immediate and painful response to an act we consider bad; sometimes it is only the smallest of twinges, even if the act is really bad; and

The extremes of penal cruelty are illustrated in this engraving from *The Terrific Register*, 1825, which depicts 'a fair criminal' being broken on the wheel in Brussels before execution by sword. She had murdered her husband for infidelity. The only concession to humanity was to lend her white satin pantaloons to cover her nakedness.

The cinematic treatment. Pola Negri, in the part of Madame Du Barry, is dragged to the guillotine. The year was 1793.

sometimes it accompanies our fantasy aggressions either as a slight ache of the spirit, or as the tearing agony of the neurotic.

Any image of executing—or punishing—a woman is therefore potentially pleasure-arousing, but also guilt-arousing, for many men. It fulfils the infantile urge latent in millions of men, both to have their own way with women, and to 'get their own back' on them; although most men would, of course, hotly deny that they had any such unholy motives. Since such urges arise in the subconscious, the sufferers are never, of course, aware of their origins.

With the majority of men, their forms of attack upon women remain devious, indirect, or symbolic; but they are nonetheless attacks; they arouse little or no sense of guilt because they are well camouflaged. But the nearer they come to overt manifestations of aggression, the more they may strike chords of guilt in the man's mind. So the contemplation of a scene displaying a woman having her head chopped off, or being hanged, is apt to arouse immediate guilt-feelings; such scenes stir direct impulses of aggression, which in turn stir feelings of guilt. It is also to be noted that the execution of a woman means she is being *punished*, and punishment re-bounds rapidly in the subconscious mind.

I once knew a very charming man in his fifties, a man especially admired by women for his extreme gentleness and courtesy, who told me that the most exciting fantasy he could conjure up was a scene where a large and arrogant woman—of young middle age with a full and luxuriant figure and a full thick neck— knelt naked, bound, and blind-folded on the scaffold, and was then beheaded by a virile and vicious Turkish executioner. I can remember his parents; the father was small and ineffectual, the mother large, handsome and domineering, who was in her thirties when he was born. His fantasy execution—which, of course, he never consciously associated in the smallest degree with his mother—included all the classic elements; she had to be of the physical and sexual type which his mother had been during the first five years of his life; she had to be as attractively and as aggressively naked as possible; she had to be bound to keep her (symbolically) from resisting; she had to be blindfolded to keep her from seeing who was executing her; and she had

finally to be rendered powerless by having her domineering head cut off.

Recently, perhaps through the loosening of restraints all round, and as a result of permissive parents acting and reacting to their children in a far more uninhibited way, the taboo of showing the execution of women seems to be breaking down; and it has started with Royalty. Within the last year or so, millions have seen on their television screens the beheading of Queens Anne Boleyn and Catherine Howard, and Mary, Queen of Scots; and, in the case of the last-named, her severed head being shown to the spectators, as in Rigaud's painting of some two hundred years ago.

Perhaps, with Women's Liberation on the way, there will soon be nothing worthy of comment when members of the female sex are shown on the scaffold being burnt, beheaded or otherwise dispatched by the executioner.

The Beheading of Saint Catherine of Alexandria, and the carrying of her body to Mount Sinai by the angels. From a watercolour by Daniel Urrabieta y Vierge (1851–1904), published in Jean Mielot's *Vie de Ste Catherine* (Paris, 1881). A pastiche, based on the style of a medieval illuminated manuscript, showing a typical execution by the sword. Urrabieta painted various scenes of the Saint's life for this elaborately printed life of Saint Catherine.

Both these illustrations purport to show the burning of Joan of Arc at Rouen on May 30, 1431. Both pictures are mid-nineteenth-century imaginative renderings of the event, and both reflect the 'idealism' of the period. The left-hand engraving, by an unknown French illustrator, shows Joan as a large matronly figure quite inappropriate to what most people have thought the Saint must have looked like; whereas the right-hand picture tries to introduce a strange and quite false sex-appeal in half stripping Joan, something which would never have happened; this is from an illustration by August Raffet (1804–60) to Anquetil's *Histoire de France* of 1852.

A seventeenth-century engraving whose origin, artist and subject-matter remain unknown. The scene shows the public beheading of an aristocratic victim. As she is crowned, and as a King stands prominently before the spectators, it is presumably the execution of a Queen. But as very few queens were executed in history, and this occasion seems not to be of any recognisable event, it may be an imaginative rendering of, perhaps, Anne Boleyn, who was beheaded with a sword in the Tower of London, but not in the presence of Henry VIII.

The execution of Lady Jane Grey on February 12, 1554. This is a detail from the highly romanticised painting by Paul Delaroche made in 1834, and now in the Guildhall Art Gallery, London. It is hard to tell why the artist placed the scene in some huge hall, whereas Jane was beheaded on Tower Hill; and why he placed the block almost on the edge of the scaffold. The figure who is guiding Jane to the block is presumably meant to be the Lieutenant of the Tower, Sir John Brydges. Although various details are quite incorrect, this picture has enjoyed a long and sustained popularity.

The execution of Mary Queen of Scots at Fotheringhay Castle on Februar

n engraving by W. N. Gardner after a painting by J. F. Rigaud, R.A. (1742–1810)

This simple little engraving is taken from *The Newgate Calendar* of 1818, and shows the cart bearing two malefactors to the gallows on February 8, 1804: they are Anne Hurle and Mathusalah Spalding. The woman was a housekeeper who defrauded her employer, and was hanged on that day for forgery, one of the many crimes then punishable by death. The man was hanged with her, his crime being 'unnatural', 'a deed without a name'. On the left is the parson who accompanied them to the scaffold. On the opposite page is another engraving, by J. Lodge, from the same edition of *The Newgate Calendar*, entitled 'The manner of burning a woman convicted of treason'. Although no name is attached to this scene, it is probably meant to represent Elizabeth Gaunt, an Anabaptist, who was burnt at Tyburn for treason (concealing rebels under Monmouth) on October 23, 1685. The general practice was to place a rope round the neck of the victim and strangle her before the flames reached her.

252

One of the most horrible incidents of the French Revolution was the cold-blooded murder of the Princesse de Lamballe. She was a very brave woman, who visited England in 1791 to raise support for the French Royal Family. She then returned to France and was imprisoned with Marie Antoinette, first in the Temple, then in La Force. On September 3, 1791, having refused to take the oath against the Monarchy, she was deliberately handed over to the mob and was torn to pieces. This engraving is by T. Wallis after W. M. Craig, and was published in 1815.

The guillotining of Queen Marie Antoinette on October 16, 1793, in the Place Louis XV. She behaved with superb dignity. This contemporary engraving shows the Queen having her arms tied behind her back before being placed on the hinged plank which shows up against the two men on her left. The plank was then tipped down and the Queen's neck securely held by the wooden lunette, the upper part of which the executioner is just about to lift to make way for the neck. The triangular blade was released by the long iron lever, which can be seen running up to its catch near the top of the blade.

President Abraham Lincoln was assassinated in Ford's Theatre in Washingon on the 14th of April 1865, and died the next day. The assassin was an actor, John Wilkes Booth, who escaped but was later run to earth and shot on the spot. Some of his fellow conspirators were caught and tried by a military tribunal. Four were sentenced to death: Lewis Paine, George Atzerodt, David Herold and Mrs Mary Surratt. Mrs Surratt kept the boarding house in which the conspiracy was hatched. Her son escaped, and others were given prison sentences. A special gallows was erected in the yard of the old Washington Penitentiary, and there, on July 7, 1865, the four were hanged, while soldiers lined the walls. On the left, Mrs Surratt is seated on a chair, her arms being bound: an umbrella is being held over her head on this extremely hot day. On the right, Mrs Surratt and Lewis Paine are seen hanging on the gallows.

On March 13, 1881, the Russian Czar Alexander II was attacked in the streets of St Petersburg by bomb-throwing Nihilists. The Czar was terribly wounded and died soon afterwards. The police rounded up six of the conspirators and their associates, and they were tried in St Petersburg in April of that year. All were found guilty and sentenced to be hanged in public. There were four men and two women, but one of these was

reprieved, as she was found to be pregnant. They were executed on April 15. Each was dressed in black, and each bore a placard on his or her chest with the one word PARRICIDE. In this woodcut, from a drawing made on the spot which appeared in the French periodical *L'Illustration* on April 30, 1881, the conspirators are seen being attended by priests before the nooses are fixed; from left to right are Kibaltchitch, Michailoff, Sophie Perowskaia, Jeliaboff, and Ryssakoff.

The execution by firing squad of the spy Mata Hari, at Vincennes, near Paris, on October 15, 1917. Mata Hari was a dancer, of Dutch origin, named Margarete Zelle, who spied for the Germans. This photograph is from a recent film of her life.